CONVERSATIONS WITH...
LEO TOLSTOY

CONVERSATIONS WITH...
LEO TOLSTOY

SIMON PARKE

Conversations with… Leo Tolstoy

White Crow Books is an imprint of
White Crow Productions Ltd
PO Box 1013
Guildford GU1 9EJ

www.whitecrowbooks.com

This edition copyright © 2009 White Crow Books

All rights reserved. Unauthorized reproduction,
in any manner, is prohibited.

Text design and eBook production by Essential Works
www.essentialworks.co.uk

ISBN 978-1-907355-25-7
eBook ISBN 978-1-907355-68-4
Audiobook ISBN 978-1-907355-46-2

Religion & Spirituality

Distributed in the UK by
Lightning Source Ltd.
Chapter House
Pitfield
Kiln Farm
Milton Keynes MK11 3LW

Distributed in the USA by
Lightning Source Inc.
246 Heil Quaker Boulevard
LaVergne
Tennessee 37086

Contents

Preface 7

Introduction 8

ONE Early Days 11

TWO Man of faith, excommunicated 27

THREE The teaching of Christ 37

FOUR Non-violence 44

FIVE Power and the military in society 53

SIX Alcohol 63

SEVEN India; and the most important thing 69

EIGHT Vegetarianism 78

NINE When the stupid rule 82

TEN Personal matters 88

ELEVEN The self-indulgent rich 93

TWELVE God? 98

THIRTEEN Writing – and the Shakespeare debate 107

FOURTEEN The end game 117

FIFTEEN What then must we do? 121

SIXTEEN The following day… 129

SEVENTEEN Afterword 130

Preface

The conversation presented here is imagined; but Tolstoy's words are not. All of Tolstoy's words included here are his own, taken from his voluminous writings.

The only alteration to his original words has been the occasional addition of a link word to help the flow. In the same cause, and for the sake of clarity, I have sometimes shortened sentences. He sometimes wrote such long and complex sentences, with numerous sub-clauses, that the casual reader is in danger of losing the thrust of the argument.

But such rare amendments never alter his meaning. After all, to discover his meaning is the reason for this adventure; so these are his passions, and his words. Yes, even the bit about him being a dirty, libidinous old man...

Introduction

Had I known what was on Tolstoy's mind as we talked, maybe I would have approached things differently; hindsight is not always a friend. But the facts are these: shortly after I saw him, he walked out on his family home of 82 years. In the early hours of October 28th 1910, under the shroud of both secrecy and darkness, he slipped away and into the night.

His first call was to visit his sister Marya – his last remaining sibling, and a nun at Sharmandino. What was his plan beyond this encounter? Some believe it was to live as religious recluse; but no one can know for sure, because he died of pneumonia on the station at Astapovo a few days later.

But this all lay in the future as my carriage approached his family estate at Yasnaya Polyana. The long and rutted drive, with trees either side, led us to the famous turret entrance, and then the house itself – a two-storey wooden building, painted white, and smaller than I imagined. Certainly not as grand as English country house; though my first memory on getting out of the coach was of family and visitors taking tea on the lawn; and all speaking English!

I was taken indoors; through the book-lined entrance hall, and then upstairs to the guest room to unpack. After this, I joined them on the lawn, waiting for the arrival of Tolstoy, who, I was told, would be joining us shortly. What did I expect?

When most think of Tolstoy, they think of the great author. *War and Peace* and *Anna Karenina* had brought him worldwide fame, universal admiration, and a good deal of money. Had he done nothing else in life, these two novels would have ensured him status and respect. Few others had written both a national epic, and a great love story; and some might have been content with that. For the last thirty years, however, Tolstoy's life has walked a different track. Since his spiritual crisis, when he was 50, he has exchanged the author's clothes for those of a prophet, and through his endless writing, has become the scourge of the rich, the Church and the Government. Neither has he missed an opportunity to denounce both science and art. Darwin? Dostoyevsky? Shakespeare? No one was to be left standing.

So who am I to meet – literary giant or savaging prophet? And is what I hear about his unhappy home life true? Things all look very peaceful here on the lawn.

And then Tolstoy emerges from the bushes, scythe in hand, sweat on his brow; and looking every inch a labourer. He has a long white beard; and wears a cap and peasant shirt, with a black belt around it. He is a shrunken figure, about 5 foot 4 inches tall. He wears a sun hat, which I became familiar with over the next few days. He would always wear it when walking in the fields. As he removes it to sit with us, I became aware of his large forehead, and thick eye brows over-hanging stern eyes.

Why am I here? He had surprisingly agreed to give some time over the next few days to talk about his life and beliefs. In many ways, it was remarkable he was still a free man, after the things he'd said about the government. But then we must remember that his full title is Count Leo Tolstoy; and privilege of birth had given him protection when criticizing government – protection that his contemporary Dostoyevsky did not receive.

For the last two decades, Tolstoy's has been the only voice in Russia which the government dared not muzzle; leaving him free to denounce a long list of perceived evils. His targets were many: the cruelty of army; the stupidity of the powerful; the unlawfulness of war; the inequality of social hierarchy; the self-indulgent behaviour of the upper classes; the oppression of poor; the immorality of the death penalty; the inadequacies of other writers; the illegality of the law courts; the demon drink and the sin of meat-eating; the evil of the church; the decline of science and art and the criminality of the censors.

His solutions to these problems lay in non-violence, God, self-control and reason.

So yes – *War and Peace* and *Anna Karenina* may have been towering achievements. But for many, Tolstoy was now a revolutionary rather than a writer; a symbol of dissent against a government which allowed no dissent; a white knight of liberty against the dead hand of bureaucratic control. Strange to say, people now loved him more for what he stood for, than for what he had written.

But what did he stand for? And more important still – who was he? Such things I hoped to discover in my conversations with... Leo Tolstoy.

ONE
Early Days

Even as an old man, Leo Tolstoy is a towering moral presence. Many had found this to be so, even if they did not agree with him. And that is my experience now, as we sit in his book-lined study, on my first morning. I have in mind the words of the artist Repin, whom I met briefly yesterday as he was leaving. He had often painted Tolstoy, and said this about him: 'Often a day or two after a conversation with him, when your mind begins to function independently, you find that you cannot agree with his views; and that some of his thoughts, which seemed at the time incontrovertible, now appear improbable.'

Would this be my experience?

SP: Your youth was a long time ago now, sir; but it is where most people start. So how do you remember your youth?

LT: At some future time I may relate the story of my life, and dwell in detail on the pathetic and instructive incidents of my youth.

SP: Your mother died when you were two, and you say that despite trying, you can gain no picture of her. But your father? I know he was often away with the pursuit of law suits; and keen also on hunting and shooting. But you were nine when he died, so there must be some memory there.

LT: I remember him in his study, when we went to say 'good night', or sometimes simply to play, where he sat on the leather divan, smoking a pipe, and caressed us, and sometimes to our great joy let us climb onto the back of the divan while he either continued to read, or talked to the clerks standing at the door, or to my godfather who often stayed with us.

SP: And of course you had three elder brothers and a sister; though only Marya is still alive now.

Tolstoy nods.

SP: And your eldest brother, Nikolay, invented an important game for you all, did he not?

LT: He did.

SP: Around the idea of the Ant Brotherhood – an imaginary community of love and happiness, who experienced no disease, trouble or anger. But you didn't as yet know the secret of this happiness – it was written on a green stick?

LT: *(Smiling)* The Ant Brotherhood was revealed to us; but not the chief secret, no – that was, the way for all men to cease suffering from any misfortune; to leave off quarrelling and being angry, and become continuously happy – this secret Nikolay said he had written on a green stick buried by the side of the road at the edge of a certain ravine near here, at which spot, since my body must be buried somewhere, I have asked to be buried – in memory of Nikolenka.

SP: You smile at the memory. But I'm aware you smile less when it comes to your later years, when you went off to Kazan University to study law and oriental languages. You came away three years later without a degree – and the suggestion was that you enjoyed wine, cards, and women a little too much!

LT: Many others must have passed through the same as I did. I honestly desired to make myself a good and virtuous man; but I was young, I had passions, and I stood alone, altogether alone, in my search after virtue. Every time I tried to express the longings of my heart for a truly virtuous life, I was met with contempt and derisive laughter. But directly I gave way

to the lowest of my passions, I was praised and encouraged!
I found ambition, love of power, love of gain, lechery, pride,
anger, vengeance, all held in high esteem. And I gave way to
these passions, and becoming like my elders, I felt that the
mark I made in the world satisfied those around me.

SP: With the death of your mother when you were so young,
you were close to your aunt, I know.

LT: My kind-hearted aunt, a really good woman, used to say
to me, that there was one thing above all others which she
wished for me – an intrigue with a married woman! *'Rien
ne forme un jeune homme, corarae une liaison avec une femme
comme il faut.'* Another of her wishes for my happiness was
that I should become an adjutant, and, if possible, to the
Emperor.

SP: Very grand.

LT: However, the greatest happiness of all for me, she thought,
would be that I should find a wealthy bride, who would bring
me as her dowry an enormous number of slaves!

SP: Well, it's a sort of happiness – but I see you shaking your
head!

LT: I cannot now recall those years without a painful feeling
of horror and loathing. I put men to death in war –

SP: You were an officer in the army, for two years –

LT: I fought duels to slay others, I lost at cards, wasted my
substance wrung from the sweat of peasants, punished the
latter cruelly, cavorted with loose women and deceived men.
Lying, robbery, adultery of all kinds, drunkenness, violence
and murder – all committed by me. I did not omit one crime

during those times – and yet I was considered by my equals a comparatively moral man! Such was my life during those years.

Oh, and during that time I began to write, of course; out of vanity, love of gain, and pride.

SP: And some of the first things you wrote were the *Sevastopol Sketches* – *Sevastopol in December* and then, *Sevastopol in May*. I noticed the second one contained a bleaker view of war; there was none of the patriotism of the first.

LT: I saw the corpses piled high in the mortuary – corpses which a couple of hours before had been men full of various lofty or trivial hopes and wishes.

Tolstoy doesn't attempt to lessen the blow; and so I allow the silence.

The hero of that tale – whom I love with all the power of my soul, and whom I tried to portray in all his beauty; who has been, is and will be beautiful – is truth.

SP: And even Tsar Nicholas I enjoyed the truth on this occasion, issuing an order of protection on your life. But you did not just write about war.

LT: I followed as a writer the same path which I had chosen as a man. In order to obtain the fame and the money for which I wrote, I was obliged to hide what was good, and bow down before what was evil. How often while writing have I cudgelled my brains to conceal under the mask of indifference or pleasantry, those yearnings for something better which formed the real problem of my life! I succeeded ill in my object, and was praised. At twenty-six years of age, on the close of the war, I came to St. Petersburg and made the acquaintance of the

Early Days

authors of the day.

SP: You are dismissive of your youth; finding no good in it. And like St. Paul in the New Testament, you keep reminding us that you were the worst of sinners!

LT: I was.

SP: Yet now things are perceived differently, by others at least. Now people come and visit you in their hundreds. They come to talk, they come to ask advice – and yes, sometimes to ask for money. I saw some of them myself yesterday. They'd travelled miles to be here, so eager to catch a glimpse of you! 'Is the great man going to show himself?' they say. For them, you are a spiritual guru.

LT: They come to see a person who has become famous for the importance and clarity of his expression of his thoughts; and yet on meeting, do not allow him to say a single word! Instead, they keep on talking, and tell him either what he has already expressed more clearly or what he long ago proved to be ridiculous!

SP: Fans are a mixed blessing, I'm sure. But from what you say, your spiritual journey has not been straightforward. Where would you say it began?

LT: I was christened and educated in the Orthodox Christian faith; I was taught it in my childhood, and in my boyhood and youth. Nevertheless, when at 18 years of age I left the university, I had discarded all belief in anything I had been taught. To judge by what I can now remember, I never had a serious belief: I merely trusted in what my elders made their profession of faith; but even this trust was very precarious.

SP: So what happened?

LT: As I have said, I lived in this senseless manner another six years, up to the time of my marriage. During this time I went abroad.

I am aware that his last trip abroad was from 1860–1861. During this time, he visited Rome and Paris again, before travelling to London where he heard Dickens read, and met the poet Matthew Arnold. He then met Proudhon in Brussels, before returning home.

LT: My life in Europe, and my acquaintance with many learned and eminent foreigners, confirmed my belief in the doctrine of general perfectibility; as I found the belief prevailed among them.

SP: The belief that the human race is evolving gradually into something better?

LT: This belief took the form which is common amongst most of the cultivated men of our day, and is expressed in the word 'progress'. It appeared to me then that this word had real meaning. I did not as yet understand that, tormented like every other man by the question 'How was I to live better?' when I answered that I must live for 'progress', I was only repeating the answer of a man carried away in a boat by the waves and wind, who to the one important question for him, 'Where are we to steer?' should answer, 'We are being carried somewhere.'

SP: Truth is the story on top, and 'perfectibility' was the story on top?

LT: I did not see this then; only at rare intervals my feelings were roused against the common superstition of our age, which leads men to ignore their own ignorance of life.

Early Days

SP: But something happened on one of your trips abroad that was to have an impact on you. In Paris, I believe?

LT: Yes, during my stay in Paris, the sight of a public execution revealed to me the weakness of my superstitious beliefs in progress.

SP: How so?

LT: When I saw the head divided from the body, and heard the sound with which it fell separately into the box, I understood, not with my reason, but with my whole being, that no theory of the wisdom of all established things, nor of progress, could justify such an act. And that if all the men in the world from the day of creation, by whatever theory, had found this thing necessary, it was a bad thing; and that therefore I must judge what was right and necessary, not by what men said and did; not by the idea of progress, but what I felt to be true in my heart.

SP: Well, we'll come back to the subject of non-violence, because it has almost become your calling card. But to return to your story – on your return to Russia – you were a teacher for a while. You started a school for the peasant children, here at Yasnaya Polyana.

LT: In reality, I was still bent on the solution of the same impossible problem – how to teach without knowing what I had to teach. Having now to deal with peasant's children, I thought I could get over this difficulty by allowing the children to learn what they liked.

SP: That all sounds very modern!

LT: It seems now absurd when I remember the expedients by which I carried out this whim of mine to teach – despite knowing in my heart that I could teach nothing useful, because I myself did not know what was necessary.

SP: 'If you don't know it yourself, then teach it to others!'

LT: After a year spent in employment with this school, I again went abroad, for the purpose of finding out how I was to teach without knowing anything.

SP: You went of an educational fact finding mission in Europe; and particularly keen on the German kindergarten, I believe. And then marriage?

LT: After I returned, I married, yes.

SP: So suddenly, a whole new set of concerns for you; and you forgot all about the execution in Paris.

LT: The new circumstances of a happy family life completely led me away from the search after the meaning of life as a whole. My life was concentrated at this time in my family – my wife and children; and consequently in the care for increasing the means of life. The effort to effect my own individual perfection – already replaced by the striving after general progress – was now changed into an effort to secure the particular happiness of my family. In this way 15 years passed.

SP: A rather remarkable fifteen years; fifteen years in which you wrote many things, but most famously, *War and Peace* and *Anna Karenina*.

LT: Yes, not withstanding the fact that during these 15 years I looked upon the craft of authorship as a very trifling thing –

SP: Really?

LT: I continued all the time to write; all the time. I experienced the seductions of authorship; the temptations of an enormous financial reward and of great applause for the valueless work, and gave myself up to it as a means of improving my material position; and of stifling in my soul all questions regarding my own life and life in general.

SP: And what, if anything, was the message of your writing at this time?

LT: I taught what for me, was the only truth – that the object of life should be our highest happiness and that of our family.

SP: And you pushed at an open door, for that is how most of us live. But something turned inside you?

LT: A strange state of mind began to grow upon me. I had moments of perplexity, of a stoppage as it were, of life; as if I did not know where to live, what I was to do. And I began to wander, and was a victim to low spirits.

SP: Strange that you felt this way at the height of your fame, when really – you had everything a man could want.

LT: Indeed. But then this state of mind passed, and I returned to living as before; until later, these periods of perplexity began to return more and more frequently, and invariably took the same form.

SP: What form was that?

LT: These stoppages of life always presented themselves to me with the same question: 'Why?' and 'What after?'

SP: Ah – death begins to question you!

LT: At first it seemed to me these were aimless and meaningless questions. It seemed to me that all they asked about was already well known; and that if at any time I wished to find answers to them, I could do so without trouble; that just at that time I could not be bothered with this – but that whenever I stopped to think them over, I'd find an answer.

SP: A perfect climate for procrastination.

LT: But these questions presented themselves to my mind with ever increasing frequency, demanding an answer with increasing persistence; and like dots grouped themselves into one black spot.

I tell you – it was with me, as happens in the case of every ailment. First appear the insignificant symptoms of illness, disregarded by the patient. Then these symptoms are repeated more and more frequently, until they merge into uninterrupted suffering. The sufferings increase, and the patient, before he has time to look around, is confronted with the fact that what he took for a mere indisposition has now become more important to him than anything on earth.

SP: So the pressure was building inside you?

LT: When considering by what means the well-being of the people might be promoted, I suddenly exclaimed: 'But what concern have I with it?' When I thought of the fame my works were gaining for me, I said to myself: 'Well, what if I should be more famous than Gogol, Pushkin, Shakespeare, Molière – than all the writers of the world – well, and what then?'…

SP: And how did you reply to yourself?

LT: I could not reply. But such questions did not wait: they demanded an immediate answer; without one it was

impossible to live; but answer there was none. I felt that
the ground on which I stood was crumbling, that there was
nothing for me to stand on; that what I had been living for
was nothing; and that I had no reason for living.

SP: Despite being more famous than Shakespeare?

LT: My life had come to a stop. I was able to breathe, to eat,
to drink, to sleep, and I could not help breathing, eating,
drinking and sleeping; but there was no real life in me because
I had not a single desire the fulfilment of which I could feel
to be reasonable. If I wished for anything, I knew beforehand
that, that were I to satisfy the wish – or were I not to satisfy it
– nothing would come of it either way.

SP: Vanity, vanity – all is vanity!

LT: The idea of suicide came as naturally as formerly, that
of bettering my life had done. Indeed, this thought was so
attractive that I was compelled to practice upon myself a
species of self-deception in order to avoid carrying it out too
speedily.

SP: You genuinely feared you would kill yourself?

LT: I was unwilling to act hastily, only because I wanted to
employ all my powers in clearing away the confusion of my
thoughts. If I should not clear them away, I could at any time
kill myself. And so here was I, a man fortunately situated,
hiding away a cord, to avoid being tempted to hang myself, by
tying it to the beam between the closets of my room, where I
undressed alone every evening. Oh, and I ceased to go hunting
with a gun because it offered too easy a way of getting rid of
life!

SP: You were in a mess.

LT: I did not know what I wanted; I was afraid of life; I struggled to get away from it, and yet all the time, there *was* something I hoped for from it.

SP: Somewhere inside a candle burned?

LT: The mental state in which I then was, seemed to me summed up in the following: my life was a foolish and wicked joke played on me by someone. Notwithstanding the fact that I did not recognize a 'someone' who may have created me, this conclusion that someone had wickedly and foolishly made a joke of me by bringing me into this world, seemed to me the most natural of all conclusions.

SP: You may have felt a joke; but you were a successful joke, and much lauded. Success blinds many to their personal needs; but not you?

LT: Under the influence of success, and flattered by praise, I had long been persuading myself that this was a work which must be done despite the approach of death, which would destroy everything – both my writings and the memory of them. But I soon saw that this was only another delusion. I saw that art is only the ornament and charm of life. And as life had lost its charm for me, how could I make others see a charm in it? Poetry and art gave me delight; it was pleasant for me to look at life in the mirror of art; but when I tried to discover the meaning of life, when I felt the necessity of living *myself*, the mirror became either unnecessary, superfluous, ridiculous or painful. I could no longer take comfort from what I saw in the mirror; my position was stupid and desperate.

SP: 'It is an unhappy business that God has given humans to be busy with,' says Solomon in the book of Ecclesiastes. 'I saw all the deeds that are done under the sun; and I see all is vanity and a chasing after the wind.'

Early Days

LT: But I asked myself this: is it possible that I have overlooked something; that I have failed to understand something? May it not be that this state of affairs is common among men?' And in every branch of human knowledge I sought an explanation of the questions that tormented me; I sought that explanation painfully and long; and not out of mere curiosity. I did not seek it indolently but painfully, obstinately, day and night; I sought it as a perishing man seeks safety; and I found nothing.

SP: I know you were a fairly voracious reader.

LT: I sought it in all branches of knowledge, and not only did I fail, but moreover, I convinced myself, that all those who searched like myself, had likewise found nothing; and had not only found nothing, but had come, as I had, to the despairing conviction that the only absolute knowledge a man can possess is this: that life is without meaning.

SP: You had reached a brick wall in yourself.

LT: The question, which in my fiftieth year had brought me to the notion of suicide, was the simplest of all questions, lying in the soul of every man, from the under-developed child to the wisest sage. And that question was as follows: 'What will come from what I am doing now, and may do tomorrow? What will come from my whole life?' Otherwise expressed, the question will be this: 'Why should I live? Why should I wish for anything? Why should I do anything?' And again, in other words, it is this: 'Is there any meaning in my life which will not be destroyed by the inevitable death awaiting me?'

SP: 'The people of long ago are not remembered; and nor will there be any remembrance of people yet to come, by those who come after them' – Solomon in Ecclesiastes again.

LT: In my search for a solution to the problem of life, I

experienced the same feeling as a man who is lost in a forest. He comes to an open plain, climbs up a tree, and sees around him a space without end, but nowhere a house. He sees clearly that there can be none; he goes into the thick of the wood, into the darkness, and sees darkness, but again no house. Thus I had lost my way in the forest of human knowledge, in the light of the mathematical and experimental sciences which opened out for me clear horizons where there could be no house, and in the darkness of philosophy, plunging me into greater gloom with every step I took, until I was at last persuaded that there was, and could be, no issue.

SP: And did you find like minds in your circle?

LT: Hardly! When I watched the narrow circle of those who were my equals in social position, I saw only people who did not understand the question; people who understood the question but kept down their understanding of it by the intoxication of life; people who understood it and put an end to life –

SP: Suicide?

LT: Of course; and finally, people who, understanding well enough, lived on in weakness, and in despair.

SP: Not a happy set of choices.

LT: And I saw no others; no others. It seemed to me that the narrow circle of learned, rich and idle people, to which I myself belonged, formed the whole of humanity, and that the millions living outside it were animals, not men.

Yes, however strange, inconceivable and improbable it now seems to me – that I could overlook the life of mankind surrounding me on all sides, and fall into such an error as to think that the life of a Solomon, a Schopenhauer and my own, was the real normal life, and that the life of unconsidered millions was a circumstance unworthy of attention – however strange this appears to me now, I see it was so.

SP: Solomon, Schopenhauer and Tolstoy. That's some company you place yourself alongside.

LT: The germs of these thoughts were already within me. I now understood that the position assumed by Solomon, Schopenhauer and myself, notwithstanding all our wisdom, was foolish: we understand that life is an evil, and yet we live. This is clearly foolish, because if life is foolish, and I care so much for reason, I should put an end to that life.

SP: Perhaps Anna Karenina was right to jump in front of the train, as she did in your novel? Life was just too foolish.

LT: Well, it is no wonder there are so many suicides when you consider how religion is so distorted, and science is such a nonsense.

SP: You blame the church and science for the glut of suicides?

LT: One of the main contributing factors to suicide in European civilization is the false church dogma about heaven and hell. People do not believe in either, but they still have the notion that life should be either heaven or hell. This idea is so ingrained in them that they cannot see life as it really is. It is neither heaven nor hell, but a constant battle – constant because life consists only of this struggle – not in the Darwinian sense against others, but a battle of spiritual forces against corporal limitations. Life is a struggle between soul and body. If life is understood in this way, suicide becomes impossible, unnecessary and senseless. One can find good only by living. If I seek good, how can I find it by exiting from life?

I want mushrooms; mushrooms are in the forest. If I want mushrooms, why would I leave the forest?

TWO
Man of faith, excommunicated

Tolstoy had finally been excommunicated by the Church in 1901; after 20 years attacking it. This event caused sensation, much sympathy, and a degree of iconization of Tolstoy in the public imagination. Repin's picture Tolstoy at Prayer *was very popular, and on sale everywhere. I have one myself: there he is, kneeling barefoot in the woods, like a latter-day St. Francis. His new book* Resurrection *came out at the same time, and caused further sensation. And I remember that Tolstoy liked his work: 'The old man wrote it well,' he said.*

In 1903, Tolstoy took further revenge on the Church in his piece: The Restoration of Hell. *The message was simple: hell was empty, until humans invented the church. It was his most devastating attack on institutional Christianity.*

So how had it all come to this? Why did this 'great sinner' first turn to the church; and then turn on the church. I was interested to find out, as we sat that evening in his study, where he seemed entirely at ease. This was his sanctuary.

SP: And so against all odds, Count, you became a man of faith? How did that happen?

LT: I was now ready to accept any faith which did not require of me a direct denial of reason; for that would be to act a lie. And I studied Buddhism and Mohammedanism in their books; and especially also Christianity, both in its writings and in the lives of its professors around me. I naturally turned my attention at first to the believers in my own immediate circle, to learned men; orthodox divines; the older monks; and to the orthodox divines of a new shade of doctrine – the so-called New Christians – who preach salvation through faith in a redeemer. I seized upon believers such as these and asked them what they believed in, and what gave them a meaning to life.

SP: And were they helpful?

LT: Despite making every possible concession and studiously avoiding all disputes – I could not accept the faith of any of these men.

SP: Why not?

LT: I saw that what they called their faith did not explain, but in fact obscured, the meaning of life; and that they professed it, not in order to answer the questions of life which had attracted me towards faith, but for some other purpose to which I was a stranger. I remember the painful feeling of horror with which I returned to the old feelings of despair, after the hopes I experienced many, many times in my relations with these people.

SP: You felt let down; or worse perhaps?

LT: I was not so much revolted by the unreasonable and unnecessary doctrines which they mingled with the Christian truths always so dear to me; as by the fact that their lives were like exactly my own! The only difference being that they did not live according to the principles they professed.

SP: Whereas you didn't have any principles to worry about.

LT: I was clearly conscious they deceived themselves, and that for them, as for myself, there was no other meaning to life than to live while they lived, and to take each for himself whatever he could lay hold on.

SP: So what happened then? Something must have changed,

for you joined this Church!

LT: I began to draw nearer to the believers among the poor, the simple and the ignorant; and the more I studied, the more I became convinced that a true faith was among them, that their faith was for them a necessary thing, and alone gave them a meaning in life and a possibility of living. In direct opposition to what I saw in our circle.

The life of the working classes; of the whole of mankind; of those that create life, appeared to me in its true significance. I understood that this was life itself, and that the meaning given to this life was true, and I accepted it.

SP: Just like that?

LT: That's right. When I remembered how these very doctrines had repelled me; how senseless they had seemed when professed by men whose lives were spent in opposition to them, and then how these same doctrines had attracted me and seemed reasonable when I saw men living in accordance with them – I understood why I had once rejected them and thought them unmeaning; and why I now adopted them and thought them full of meaning. I understood that I had erred, and how I had erred. I had erred, not so much through having thought incorrectly, as having lived ill.

I note that Tolstoy is proud of his thinking, but remain quiet for the time being, as he is visibly disturbed if it is questioned. He continues:

LT: Now if the question, 'What is life?' were asked of himself by the executioner, who passes his life in torturing and cutting off heads, or by a confirmed drunkard, or by a crazy man who has spent his whole life in a darkened chamber, hating that chamber, and imagining he would perish if he left it – then evidently he could get no other answer to his question, 'What is Life?' than that life is the greatest of evils; and the crazy man's answer would be a true one, but only for himself. Here then, was I such a crazy man? Were all of us rich, clever, idle men, crazy like this?

SP: And were you?

LT: Well, I understood at last that we actually were; that I, at any rate, was. In fact, the bird is so constituted that it must fly, pick up its food, build its nest; and when I see the bird doing this I rejoice in its joy. What then must man do? He must also gain his living like the animals, but with this difference, that he will perish if he attempt it alone; he must labour not for himself, but for all. And when he does so, I am firmly convinced he is happy, and his life is reasonable.

SP: And you weren't happy because you had not lived in this way?

LT: What had I done during my thirty years of conscious life? I had not only not helped the life of others; I had done nothing for my own. I had lived the life of a parasite, and when I asked myself why I lived at all I received the answer, 'There is no reason why.' My life was an evil and an absurdity.

SP: Your inner life at this time sounds like a battle ground; a struggle for some sort of justification or purpose to save you from your self-loathing. Is this when God appeared?

LT: I do not live when I lose faith in the existence of a God. I should long ago have killed myself if I had not had a dim hope of finding Him. I really live only when I am conscious of him and seek him. 'What more then do I seek?' I asked myself. And a voice seemed to cry within me, 'This is He; He without whom there is no life. To know God and to live are one. God is life.'

SP: Suddenly you were certain?

LT: Live to seek God and life will not be without God. And stronger than ever life rose up in and around me; and the light that then shone never left me again. Thus I was saved from self-murder. When and how this change in me took place, I could not say. As gradually and imperceptibly as life had decayed in me, till I reached the impossibility of living; till life stood still, and I longed to kill myself – so gradually and imperceptibly I felt the glow and strength of life return to me. And strangely enough, this power of life which came back to me was not new; it was old enough, for I had been led by it in the earlier part of my life. I returned as it were, to the past; to childhood and my youth. I returned to the belief that the one single aim of life should be to become better; that is, to live in accordance with that will.

SP: And so now you, dissolute Leo Tolstoy, had become a man of faith? Quite a change!

LT: The position which I occupied in relation to questions of faith had become quite different from what it once was. Formerly, life itself had seemed to be full of meaning, and faith an arbitrary assertion of certain useless and unreasonable propositions which had no direct bearing on life. I had tried to find out their meaning; and once convinced they had none, had thrown them aside. Now, on the contrary, I knew for certain that the propositions of faith not only appeared no longer useless to me, but had been shown beyond dispute by my own experience to be that which alone gave a meaning to life. Formerly, I had looked on them as a worthless illegible scrawl; but now if I did not understand them, still I knew that they had a meaning, and I said to myself that I must learn to understand them.

SP: And so you sought out new tutors. You knocked on the door of the Orthodox Church and asked for their guidance.

LT: According to the explanation of these divines, the fundamental dogma of faith is the infallibility of the church.

SP: The idea that the church cannot be wrong.

LT: And from the acceptance of this dogma follows, as a necessary consequence, the truth of everything that is taught by the church. The Church, as the assembly of believers united in love, and consequently possessing true knowledge, became the foundation of my faith. I said to myself: 'Divine truth cannot be obtained by any one man; it can be reached only by the union of all men through love. In order to attain the truth, we must not go each his own way; and, to avoid division, we must have love one another, and bear with things we do not agree with. Truth is revealed in love, and therefore, if we do not obey the ordinances of the church, we destroy love; but if love is destroyed we are deprived of the possibility of knowing the truth.'

SP: That's quite a net to throw over believers: keeps everyone together and allows little room for individual movement!

LT: Indeed. And while fulfilling the ordinances of the church, I submitted my reason to the tradition adopted by the mass of my fellow men. I united myself to my ancestors – to those I loved – my father, mother and grand parents. They and all before them lived and believed and brought me into being. I joined the millions of people who I respect. And there was nothing bad in all this; for bad for me meant the indulgence of the lusts of the flesh. When I got up early to attend divine service, I knew that I was doing well, if it were only because I tamed my intellectual pride for the sake of a closer union with my ancestors and contemporaries; and, in order to seek for a meaning in life, sacrificed my bodily comfort.

SP: It was a great act of submission on your part; both intellectual and emotional. Yet history records that soon you began to feel uncomfortable. When did you first notice this feeling?

LT: This feeling came upon me the strongest whenever I took part in the most ordinary, and generally considered the most important sacraments, of christening and the Holy Communion. Here I no interest in anything incomprehensible, but rather, with what was easy to understand. So such acts appeared to me a delusion, and I was on the horns of a dilemma – to lie or to reject?

SP: So you did not accept the church's teaching about the bread and wine literally becoming the body and blood of Christ?

LT: I shall never forget the painful feeling I experienced when I took the communion for the first time after many years. When I drew near to the 'the holy gates', and the priest called on me to repeat that I believed that what I was about to swallow was the real body and blood – it cut me to the heart. It was a false note, though small; here was no unconsidered word, but a cruel demand of one who had evidently never known what faith was.

SP: It must have been difficult for you, when the central act of Christian worship forced you either to lie to yourself or reject it. Did you leave the church immediately?

LT: Not immediately. Notwithstanding all my doubts and sufferings, I still clung to Orthodoxy for a while; but practical questions arose and had to be settled, and the decisions concerning these questions by the church, contrary to the elementary principles of the faith by which I lived, compelled me finally to abandon all communion with it.

SP: What questions were these?

LT: The questions were, in the first place, the relationship of the Orthodox church to other churches, to Catholicism and the so-called Raskolniks or Dissenters. I desired to be a brother to these men, and what came of it? The doctrines which had seemed to promise me the union of all men in one faith and love – these doctrines, in the persons of their best representatives, told me that all these other people were living in a lie!

SP: So the Orthodox Church wouldn't acknowledge the validity of any other church? They are hardly alone in that, of course; soft walls of separation do tend to harden over the years.

LT: This is true. Clergymen of all the different religions, the best representatives of them, without exception, all told me of their belief that they alone were right; and all others were wrong! And that all they could do for those in error was to pray for them!

SP: But we rarely do things for one single reason, do we? Our decisions are usually a composite of circumstances. And surely it wasn't just the Holy Communion that drove you from the Church?

LT: No. The second point which concerned the relationship of the church to the problems of life was her connection with war and executions.

SP: Of course you were a soldier once yourself, at the age of 24; and even then you wrote that all war was unjust. So these things had been simmering in you for a while.

LT: Maybe. Certainly at this time Russia was engaged in war, and, in the name of Christian love, Russians were engaged in slaying their brethren.

SP: And you weren't happy with this.

LT: Not to regard this as impossible; not to see that murder is evil, contrary to the very first principles of every faith, was impossible. But at the same time in the churches, men were praying for the success of our arms, and the teachers of religion were accepting these murders as acts which were the consequence of faith! Not only murder in actual warfare was approved, but during the troubles which ensued, I saw members of the church, her teachers, monks and ascetics, approving of the murder of erring and helpless youths. I looked around on all that was done by men who professed to be Christians, and I was horrified.

SP: It seems to me that whatever you think of the church, it has a difficult job. It has to both maintain an ideal, whilst also working with what is; with the reality on the ground. People are violent, manipulative and cunning and no amount of wishing will make it otherwise. So isn't talk of non-violence – as preached by Jesus in the Sermon on the Mount – just a distant and impossible dream?

LT: The least that can be asked of any men who pass judgement upon any doctrine, is that they understand it as the teacher himself understood it. Jesus understood his doctrine not as some distant ideal, impossible to attain; nor as a collection of fantastic and poetical reveries with which to charm the simple-hearted in habitants of Galilee. He understood it as reality – a reality which should be the salvation of mankind. He was not dreaming as he hung on the cross, but he cried out and died for his doctrine. And thus many men died and still die. It is impossible to say that such a doctrine is a dream.

SP: Perhaps it is a dream; but a dream worth dying for.

LT: The advance of humanity towards righteousness is due not to the tyrants but to the martyrs. As fire cannot extinguish fire, so evil cannot extinguish evil. Only good, confronting evil and resisting its contagion, can overcome evil. And in the inner world of the human soul, the law is as absolute as was even the law of Galileo; more absolute, more clear, more immutable.

THREE

The teaching of Christ

Tolstoy's book The Kingdom of God is Within You *– is both an idealistic call to accept peaceful values of Christ; and a disturbing reminder that all power is essentially violent. Tolstoy's Christ is a neutered Christ; human and reasonable. Here is no supernatural figure, terrifying in judgement. Rather, he is a man challenging people with reason – which of course is how Tolstoy saw his own mission.*

I'm aware that Tolstoy's creed was a simple affair, gleaned from the 'Sermon on the Mount'. It had five propositions: 1) Love your enemies 2) Do not be angry 3) Do not lust 4) Do not fight evil with evil and 5) Do not take oaths.

It was, in a way, his own religion. But how had he come to it? We are sitting on a bench in the garden. Despite his age, Tolstoy is eager to be out on the land. But has granted me a little time.

SP: You claim that there was a moment when Christ's teaching appeared as new to you.

LT: That is correct.

SP: Yet how could this be, given that you were soaked in it from your childhood?

LT: What was new? The true meaning of Christ's teaching was revealed to me; and everything confirmed its truth. For a long time, of course, I could not accustom myself to the strange idea; that after the eighteen centuries during which Christ's law had been professed by millions of human beings; after thousands of men had consecrated their lives to the study of this law, I had actually discovered it for myself as something new!

SP: But as I say, you knew it already.

LT: Indeed. When I began to read the Gospel, I was not in the condition of a man who, having heard nothing of Christ's teaching, becomes acquainted with it for the first time. On the contrary, I had a preconceived theory as to the manner in which I ought to understand it. Christ did not appear to me as a prophet revealing the divine law, but as one who continued and amplified the absolute divine law which I already knew. I had very definite and complex notions about God, about the creation of the world and of man, and about the commandments of God given to men through the instrumentality of Moses.

SP: So instead of coming to Christ with fresh eyes, you came with what you now perceive as the unhelpful baggage of the Old Testament?

LT: If I had simply referred to Christ's teaching without the theological theory that I had imbibed with my mother's milk, I should simply have understood the simple meaning of Christ's words. I should have understood that Christ abolished the old law, and gave a new law. But I had been taught that Christ did not abolish the old law, but that on the contrary, he confirmed it to the slightest iota, and that he made it more complete. But now I understood the simple and clear meaning of Christ's teaching, I saw clearly that the two laws are directly opposed to one another; that they can never be harmonized; and that instead of supplementing one by the other, we must inevitably choose between the two.

SP: Christ says, in Matthew 5. Verse 17, that he has not come to destroy the law –

LT: The eternal law; he has not come to destroy the eternal law. In effect, Christ says: 'I am not come to destroy the eternal law of whose fulfilment your books and prophecies foretell. I am come to teach you the fulfilment of the eternal law; not of the law your scribes and Pharisees call the divine law, but of that eternal law which is less subject to change than the earth and the heavens.'

SP: That is your understanding?

LT: I have expressed the idea in other words in order to detach your thoughts from the traditional interpretation. If this false interpretation had never existed –

SP: – that Christ was just fulfilling something already started by Moses and the prophets –

LT: – then the idea expressed by Jesus could not be rendered in a better or more definitive manner. Christ recognized the Mosaic law, and still more the prophets –

SP: – but only in so much as they reflected the eternal law; and when they do not, he places his own law above them; while the church tries to blend them together.

LT: The impossible attempts by the church to reconcile the irreconcilable is not just an error of thought, but has a clear and definite object.

SP: To maintain things as they are?

LT: Instead of recognizing as divine truth one or other of the two laws, the law of Moses' or Christ's, *both* are considered divine. But when the question touches the acts of every day life, Christ's law is rejected and that of Moses is followed. And in this false interpretation, when we realize its importance, is the source of that terrible, that horrible drama of the struggle between good and evil, between darkness and light.

And this is why after eighteen hundred years, it so singularly happened that I discovered the meaning of Christ's teaching as something new.

SP: You didn't so much discover it; as found it already there.

LT: True. I did not discover it. I did simply what all men have done and must do who seek after God and his law; I found what is the eternal law of God.

SP: So let us talk about Christ's new commands. I always imagined that his new way was to reduce the ten commandments to just two – love God, and love your neighbour. But you don't agree, do you?

LT: Throughout the gospels it speaks of Christ's commands and the necessity of practicing them. All the theologians discuss Christ's commands; but I did not before know what those commands were. I thought, as you say, that Christ's command consisted in loving God, and one's neighbour as oneself. I did not see that this could not be Christ's command since it had already been given in Deuteronomy and Leviticus.

SP: And so because they are not new – because someone else had used the idea – then it's your belief that these commands cannot be at the heart of Christ's teaching?

LT: It became evident to me that if the gospels had come down to us half-burned or effaced, it would have been easier to restore the true meaning of the text than to find that meaning now, beneath the accumulations of fallacious comments which have apparently no purpose save to conceal the doctrine they are supposed to expound!

SP: So is there truth in the gospels? And if so, what sort?

The teaching of Christ

LT: The truth is there for all who will read the Gospels with a sincere wish to know the truth, without prejudice, and, above all, without supposing that the Gospels contain some special sort of wisdom beyond human reason.

SP: No supernatural happenings like miracles or resurrections?

LT: That is how I read the Gospels, and I found in them truth plain enough for little children to understand, as, indeed, the Gospels themselves say. So that when I am asked what my teaching consists in, and how I understand Christ's teaching, I reply: I have no teaching, but I understand Christ's teaching as it is explained in the Gospels. If I have written books about Christ's teaching, I have done so only to show the falseness of the interpretations given by the commentators on the Gospels.

SP: So how are we to read the gospels?

LT: To understand Christ's real teaching the chief thing is not to interpret the Gospels, but to understand them as they are written. And, therefore, to the question how Christ's teaching should be understood, I reply: If you wish to understand it, read the Gospels. Read them putting aside all foregone conclusions; read with the sole desire to understand what is said there. But notwithstanding the fact that they are holy books, read them considerately, reasonably, and with discernment; and not haphazardly or mechanically, as if all the words were of equal weight.

SP: Some parts are more important than others?

LT: To understand any book one must choose out the parts that are quite clear, dividing them from what is obscure or confused. And from what is clear we must form our idea of the drift and spirit of the whole work. Then, on the basis of what we have understood, we may proceed to make out what is confused or not quite intelligible. That is how we read all kinds of books. And it is particularly necessary thus to read the Gospels, which have passed through such a multiplicity of compilations, translations, and transcriptions, and were composed, eighteen centuries ago, by men who were not highly educated, and were superstitious.

No – in order to understand the Gospels, we must first of all separate what is quite simple and intelligible from what is confused and unintelligible, and afterward read this clear and intelligible part several times over, trying fully to assimilate it. It is just this that is fully comprehensible to all men that constitutes the essence of Christ's teaching.

SP: So you feel able to become the arbiter of what is, and what is not important?

LT: The Gospels, as is known to all who have studied their origin, far from being infallible expressions of divine truth, are the work of innumerable minds and hands, and are full of errors. Therefore the Gospels can in no case be taken as a production of the Holy Ghost, as Churchmen assert. Were that so, God would have revealed the Gospel as he is said to have revealed the commandments on Mount Sinai; or he would have transmitted the complete book to men, as the Mormons declare was the case with their holy scriptures. But we know how these works were written and collected, and how they were corrected and translated; and therefore not only can we not accept them as infallible revelations, but we must, if we respect truth, correct errors that we find in them.

SP: But Christ's teachings, as you found them – they inspired you?

LT: The follower of Christ's teaching is like a man carrying a lantern in front of him on a stick which might be long or short; the light is always in front of him, and is always inciting him to follow. And then it opens up to him a new space ahead, filled with light, and drawing the man to itself.

FOUR

Non-violence

In the break between conversations, I read the Catechism of Non-Resistance *by Adin Ballou, which Tolstoy quotes favourably in* The Kingdom of God is Within You. *It makes interesting reading.*

Q: Whence is the word 'non-resistance' derived?

A: From the command 'Resist not evil'.

Q: What does this word express?

A: It expresses a lofty Christian value enjoined on us by Christ.

Q: Ought the word 'non-resistance' to be taken in its widest sense – that is to say, as intending we should not offer any resistance to any kind of evil?

A: No, it ought to be taken in the exact sense of our saviour's teaching – that is, not repaying evil for evil. We ought to oppose evil by every righteous means in our power, but not by evil.

Q: What is there to show that Christ enjoined evil in that sense?

A: It is shown by the words he uttered at the same time. He said 'You have heard that it was said an eye for an eye, and a tooth for a tooth. But I say unto you, resist not evil. If one smites thee on the left cheek, turn him the other also; and if someone goes to court to get your coat, then give him your cloak also. Noah, Moses and the prophets taught that the evil doer must be punished with death; wrong must be opposed by wrong, murder by murder, evil with evil. But Christ rejects all this.

Q: May he someone kill or maim in self-defence?

A: No

Q: May he go with a complaint to the judge that he who has wronged him may be punished?

A: No. What he does through others he is in reality doing himself.

Q: Can he fight in conflict with foreign enemies or disturbers of the peace?

A: Certainly not. He cannot take any part in war or in preparation for war.

Q: Can he voluntarily give money to aid a government resting on military force, capital punishment or violence in general?

A: No. Unless the money is destined for some special object, right in itself, and good both in aims and means.

Q: Can he pay taxes to such a government?

A: No, he ought not voluntarily to pay taxes, but he ought not to resist the collecting of taxes.

Q: Can a Christian give a vote at elections, or take part in government or law business?

A: No, participation in election, government or law business is participation in government by force.

Q: Wherein lies the chief significance of the doctrine of non-resistance?

A: In the fact that it alone allows the possibility of eradicating evil from one's own heart, and also from one's neighbour's. True non-resistance is the only real resistance to evil. It is crushing the serpent's head. It destroys, and in the end extirpates, the evil feeling.

Q: But can it always be put into practice?

A: It can be put into practice like every virtue enjoined by the law of God. A virtue cannot be practiced in all circumstances without self-sacrifice, privation, suffering and in extreme cases, loss of life itself. Non-resistance is salvation; resistance is ruin.

Q: But if only a few act like this – what will happen to them?

A: If only one man acted thus, and all the rest agreed to crucify him, would it not be nobler for him to die in the glory of non-resisting love, praying for his enemies, than to live to wear the crown of Caesar stained with the blood of the slain?

Adin Ballou died in 1850. He had written about non-resistance for 50 years, yet I had never heard of him. Tolstoy angrily shakes his head as I reveal this, and tells me that Ballou's obituaries mention nothing of his pacifism; not a thing.

LT: It just seems as though it did not exist and never had existed.

SP: So do men who hold this creed get put to death here?

LT: To put a man openly to death because he believes in the creed we all confess, is impossible. And so all kinds of shifts and wiles are set on foot against him. They either send him to

Non-violence

the frontier or provoke him to insubordination. They sent one man to Tashkend; that is, they pretended to transfer him to the Tashkend army. Another, they sent to the lunatic asylum.

SP: It sounds like your voice is not heard by those holding power.

LT: Not only the government, but the great majority of liberal, advanced people, as they are called, studiously turn away from everything that has been written or done, or is being done by men, to prove the incompatibility of force in its most awful, gross and glaring form – of an army of soldiers prepared to murder anyone, whoever it may be – with the teachings of Christianity; or even of the humanity which society professes as its creed.

SP: Even if you have never fought in one, there are those who believe in 'just' wars.

LT: To destroy another life for the sake of justice is as though a man, to repair the misfortune of losing one arm, should cut off the other for the sake of equity.

SP: I take your point. But what then is the basis of society today?

LT: After much thought, what became obvious to me was this: that the organization of our society rests, not as people interested in maintaining the present order of things like to imagine, on certain principles of jurisprudence – but rather, on simple brute force; on the murder and torture of men.

SP: And the alternative is?

LT: Very early – thousands of years before our time – amid this life based on coercion, one and the same thought constantly emerged among different nations, namely, that in every individual, a spiritual element is manifested that gives life to all that exists; and that this spiritual element strives to unite with everything of a like nature to itself; achieving this aim through love.

SP: Where did this sense emerge from?

LT: This thought appeared in most various forms at different times and places, with varying completeness and clarity. It found expression in Brahmanism, Judaism, Mazdaism (the teachings of Zoroaster), in Buddhism, Taoism, Confucianism, and in the writings of the Greek and Roman sages, as well as in Christianity and Mohammedanism. The mere fact that this thought has sprung up among different nations and at different times, indicates that it is inherent in human nature and contains the truth.

SP: So why has it failed?

LT: This truth was made known to people who considered that a community could only be kept together if some of them restrained others; and so of course it appeared quite irreconcilable with the existing order of society. Moreover, it was at first expressed only fragmentarily, and so obscurely that though people admitted its theoretical truth, they could not entirely accept it as guidance for their conduct.

SP: It was somehow too frail as an idea; too elusive.

LT: Then, too, the dissemination of the truth in a society based on coercion was always hindered in one and the same manner. Those in power, feeling that recognition of this truth would undermine their position, consciously – or sometimes unconsciously – perverted it by explanations and additions quite foreign to it; and also opposed it by open violence. Thus the truth – that his life should be directed by the spiritual element which is its basis, which manifests itself as love, and which is so natural to man – this truth, in order to force a way to man's consciousness, had to struggle not merely against the obscurity with which it was expressed, and the intentional and unintentional distortions surrounding it; but also against deliberate violence, which by means of persecutions and punishments, sought to compel men to accept religious laws authorized by the rulers, and conflicting with the truth.

SP: And this repression was world-wide?

LT: Such a hindrance and misrepresentation of the truth – which had not yet achieved complete clarity – occurred everywhere: in Confucianism and Taoism, in Buddhism and in Christianity, in Mohammedanism and in Brahmanism.

SP: And how is this violence justified by those who perpetrate it?

LT: In former times the chief method of justifying the use of violence and thereby infringing the law of love, was by claiming a divine right for the rulers: the Tsars, Sultans, Rajahs, Shahs, and other heads of states. But of course the longer humanity lived the weaker grew the belief in this peculiar, God-given right of the ruler.

SP: And now?

LT: The most widespread justification is, at bottom, the age-old religious one just a little altered: that in public life, the suppression of some, for the protection of the majority, cannot be avoided. And so coercion is reckoned unavoidable – however desirable reliance on love alone might be in human intercourse. The only difference in this justification by pseudo-science consists in the fact that, to the question why such and such people and not others have the right to decide against whom violence may and must be used, pseudo-science now gives a different reply to that given by religion. Religion declared that the right to decide was valid because it was pronounced by persons possessed of divine power. Science says that these decisions represent the will of the people, which under a constitutional form of government, is supposed to find expression in all the decisions and actions of those who are at the helm at the moment.

SP: The divine right of democracy!

LT: Such are the scientific justifications of the principle of coercion. They are not merely weak but absolutely invalid; yet they are so much needed by those who occupy privileged positions, that they believe in them as blindly as they formerly believed in the Immaculate Conception; and propagate them just as confidently. And the unfortunate majority of labouring men are so dazzled by the pomp with which these 'scientific truths' are presented, that under this new influence, it accepts these scientific stupidities for holy truth; just as it formerly accepted the pseudo-religious justifications. And so they continue to submit to the present holders of power who are just as hard-hearted but rather more numerous than before.

SP: So tell me, sir – how should it be?

LT: Let me tell you a story; a true one. I once took part in Moscow in a religious meeting in the week after Easter near the church in Obotny Row. A little knot of some twenty men were gathered together on the pavement, engaged in serious theological discussion.

SP: A fine picture in itself!

LT: A police officer noting this little group sent a mounted policeman to disperse it. It was absolutely unnecessary for the officer to disperse it. A group of twenty men was an obstruction to no one, but he'd been standing there for the whole morning, and wanted something to do. The police man, a young fellow, with a resolute flourish of his right arm and a clink of his sabre, came up to us and commanded us severely: 'Move On! What's the meeting about?' One of the speakers, a quiet man in peasant's dress, answered with a calm and gracious air: 'We are speaking of serious matters, and there is no need for us to move on; you would do better, young man, to get off your horse and listen. It might do you good,' and turning round, he continued his discourse. The police man turned his horse and went off without a word!

SP: Truth peacefully prevailed.

LT: This is just what should be done in all case of violence. The officer was bored, he had nothing to do. He had been put, poor fellow, in a position in which he had no choice but to give orders. He was shut off from all human existence; he could do nothing but superintend and give orders, and give orders and superintend, though his superintendence and his orders served no useful purpose whatsoever. And this is the position in which all these unlucky rulers, ministers, members of parliament, governors, generals, officers, archbishops, priests and even rich men find themselves to some extent already; and will find themselves altogether as time goes on. They can do nothing but give orders, and they give orders and send their messengers to interfere with people. And because the people they hinder turn to them and request them not to interfere, they fancy they are very useful indeed. But the time is coming when all institutions based on force will disappear through their uselessness, stupidity and even inconvenience becoming obvious to all.

Tolstoy seems restless, and is ushering me to the door of his study, as he makes to leave. His final words are spoken across the hall:

LT: A man is considered a disgrace if he is accused of theft, brawling or not paying card debts etc, but not if he signs a death sentence, takes part in an execution, reads other people's letters, separates fathers and husbands and wives from their families, confiscates people's resources, or puts them in prison. But surely that is worse?!

FIVE
Power and the military in society

At the age of 24, Tolstoy had himself been a soldier. His brilliantly observed Sevastopol Sketches *brought war to life, with* Sevastopol in December *followed by the bleaker,* Sevastopol in May. *Even back then, he had written that since war was unjust, those involved in war must stifle their consciences, in order to survive. Later in life, this anti-war attitude hardened; and for change to come, he believed things had to be called by their right name: an army was an instrument of killing; and the enrolment and management of an army, nothing less than preparation for murder.*

The Crimean War, in which Tolstoy fought, was reckoned by many to be entirely avoidable and pointless. Had he experienced a nobler war, is it possible his views would be different? I hope to find out now.

SP: You can see an army as nothing other than an instrument of oppression?

LT: Just as a trained tiger – who does not eat meat put under his nose and jumps over a stick at a word of command – does not act thus because he likes it, but because he remembers the red hot irons or the fast with which he was punished every time he did not obey; so men submitting to what is disadvantageous or even ruinous to them, and considered by them as unjust, act thus because they remember what they suffered for resisting it.

SP: We act only out of fear?

LT: As for those who profit by the privileges gained by previous acts of violence, they often forget and like to forget how these privileges were obtained. But one need only recall the acts of history; not the history of the exploits of different dynasties of rulers, but real history – the history of the oppression of the majority by a small number of men – to see that all the advantages the rich have over the poor are based on nothing but flogging, imprisonment and murder.

SP: Which reminds me of the time you met a group of soldiers who were off to punish some peasants who had stood up to a landowner in the province of Orel. You watched the soldiers as they prepared to set off and found it most disturbing.

LT: All these men – who were going to murder or to torture the famishing and defenceless creatures who provide them with their sustenance – had the air of men who knew very well that they were doing their duty. Some were even proud and glorying in what they were doing.

SP: So what had happened?

LT: All these people were within half an hour of reaching the place where – in order to provide a wealthy young man with three thousand roubles stolen from a community of starving peasants – they'd be forced to perform the most horrible acts one can imagine; to murder or torture – as would be done in Orel – innocent beings, their brothers. And to see them approach the whole affair with untroubled serenity!

SP: Maybe they didn't know what they were going to do.

LT: To say that all these government officials, officers and soldiers did not know what was before them is impossible; for they were prepared for it. The governor must have given orders about the rods; the officials must have ordered them, paid for them, and entered the items in their accounts. They all knew that they were going to torture, perhaps to kill, their hungry fellow creatures; and that they must set to work within the hour.

SP: Well then, perhaps they were just a bad bunch?

Tolstoy shakes his head.

LT: I know these men. If I don't know them personally, I know their characters pretty clearly; their past and their way of thinking. They certainly all have mothers, some of them wives and children. They are certainly for the most part good, kind, even tender-hearted fellows, who hate every sort of cruelty not to speak of murder; many of them would not kill or hurt an animal.

SP: So it's just the common man earning a wage; and not caring too much how they do it.

LT: But it is not only these men going by train, prepared for murder and torture. How could the men who began the whole business – the landowner, the commissioner, the judges and those who gave the order and are responsible for it, the ministers, the tsar, who are also good men and professed Christians – how could they elaborate such a plan and assent to it, knowing its consequences?

SP: Did the other onlookers have an opinion?

LT: The spectators looked with sympathy rather than disapproval at all these people preparing to carry out this infamous action. In the same compartment with me was a wood merchant, who had risen from a peasant. He openly expressed his sympathy with such punishments. 'They can't disobey the authorities,' he said; 'that's what the authorities are for. Let them have a lesson; send their fleas flying! They'll give over making commotions, I warrant you!'

It's not possible to say that all those who have provoked or aided or allowed this deed are such worthless creatures. All of them in certain circumstances know how to stand up for their principles. Not one of these officials would steal a purse, read another man's letter, or put up with an affront without demanding satisfaction. Not one of these officers would consent to cheat at cards; would refuse to pay a debt of honour, would betray a comrade, run away on the battle field or desert the flag. Not one of these soldiers would spit out the holy sacrament or eat meat on Good Friday. They each have the resolve to resist acting against their principles.

SP: But they don't. So why is that?

LT: All the deeds of violence by tyrants – from Napoleon to the lowest commander of a company who fires on a crowd – can only be explained by the intoxicating effect of their absolute power over these slaves. All force, therefore, rests on the shoulders of those who carry out the deeds of violence with their own hands; that is, the men who serve in the police or the army – especially the army, for the police only venture to do their work, because the army is at their back.

SP: But what of the masses who do their work for them – yet gain nothing from it?

LT: You mean what has bought them to accept the amazing delusion that the existing order, unprofitable, ruinous and fatal as it is for them – is the order which ought to exist?

SP: Exactly.

LT: Simple. They cannot imagine that the leaders of civilization, the educated classes, could so confidently preach two such opposed principles as the law of Christ and murder. A simple uncorrupted youth cannot imagine that those who stand so high in his opinion, whom he regards as holy or learned men, could for any object whatever, mislead him so shamefully. The general delusion is diffused among the population by means of the catechism; or books in use for the compulsory education of children. In them it is stated that violence – that is, imprisonment and execution, as well as murder in civil or foreign war in the defence and maintenance of the existing state organization – is absolutely lawful and not opposed to morality and Christianity.

SP: And isn't it true that a priest actually oversees the soldiers taking the oath?

LT: The police clear a way for him through the crowd! It is the 'reverend father' come to administer the oath. And this father, who has been persuaded that he is specially and exclusively devoted to the service of Christ; and who, for the most part, does not himself see the deception in which he lives, goes into the hall where the conscripts are waiting. He throws round him a kind of curtain of brocade, pulls his long hair out over it, opens the very gospel in which swearing is forbidden, takes the cross – the very cross on which Christ was crucified because he would not do what this false servant of his is telling men to do – and puts them on the lectern. And all these unhappy, defenceless and deluded lads repeat after him the lie, which he utters with the assurance of familiarity.

SP: And then what?

LT: He reads, and they repeat after him: 'I promise and swear by Almighty God upon his holy gospel' etc. etc. 'to defend' etc. and that is to murder anyone I am told to, and to do everything I am told by men I know nothing of, and who care nothing for me except as an instrument for perpetrating the crimes by which they are kept in their position of power; and my brothers in their condition of misery. All the conscripts repeat these ferocious words without thinking. And then the so-called 'father' goes away with a sense of having correctly and conscientiously done his duty.

SP: So are soldiers told that God is the ultimate authority when making decisions?

LT: In Article 88 of the military instructions, it says a subordinate ought never to refuse to carry out an order except when he sees clearly that in carrying out his superior's command, he breaks – and yes, one expects it to say the law of God, but not at all – *his oath of fidelity and allegiance to the Tsar!* Hah!

SP: Yes, well I too am surprised. But that done, they then join the army?

LT: For two or three weeks, they go on living at home, and most of that time they are 'jaunting', that is, drinking. On a fixed day they collect them, drive them together like a flock of sheep, and begin to train them in military exercises and drill. Their teachers are fellows like themselves, only deceived and brutalized two or three years earlier. The means of instruction are: deception, stupefaction, blows and vodka. And before a year has passed, these good, intelligent, healthy minded lads will be as brutal beings as their instructors.

SP: And you believe that putting such power in the hands of authority is not just immoral and evil – but actually unsafe.

LT: What are people thinking about? I don't mean Christians, priests, philanthropists and moralists; but simply people who value their life, their security and their comfort. We know the organization will work just as well in one man's hands as another's. Today, let us assume, power is in the hands of a ruler who can be endured; but tomorrow it may be seized by a

Biron, an Elizabeth, a Catherine, a Pougachef, a Napoleon I or Napoleon III! And the man in authority, endurable today, may become a brute tomorrow; or may be succeeded by a mad or imbecile heir, like the King of Bavaria or our own Paul 1st.

SP: But so much paper shuffling goes on it's sometimes hard to know who is responsible for things done.

LT: In ancient times, tyrants got credit for the crimes they committed; but in our day, the most atrocious infamies, inconceivable under the Neros, are perpetrated and as you say, no one gets blamed for them. One set of people have suggested the idea, and other set have proposed, a third have reported back, a fourth have taken the decision, a fifth have confirmed it, a sixth have given the order and a seventh have carried it out! They hang; they flog women to death as was done recently among us in Russia at the Yuzovsky factory. And such things are being done everywhere in Europe and America in the struggle with the anarchists, and all other rebels against the existing order. They shoot and hang men by hundreds and thousands; or massacre millions in war; or break men's hearts in solitary confinement, and ruin their souls in the corruption of a soldier's life – and no one is responsible. No one!

SP: And the climate of inequality, whereby it's accepted by all that some must be elevated, and others degraded. It is an insanity everyone is blind to?

LT: Indeed. Those in whom the idea has been instilled that they are invested with a special supernatural grandeur and consequence, are so intoxicated with a sense of their own imagined dignity, that they cease to feel responsibility for what they do. While those, on the other hand, in whom the idea is fostered that they are inferior animals, bound to obey their superiors in everything, fall – through this endless humiliation – into a strange condition of stupefied servility; and in this state, of course, do not see the significance of their actions; and lose all consciousness of responsibility for what they do.

SP: Power is an intoxicating brew.

LT: And under the influence of this intoxication, men imagine themselves no longer simply men as they are, but some special beings – noblemen, merchants, governors, judges, officers, tsars, ministers or soldiers – no longer bound by ordinary human duties, but by other duties, far more weighty. Thus the landowner who claimed the forest in Orel, acted as he did only because he reckoned himself to be not an ordinary man, having the same rights to life as the peasants living next door to him; but a great land owner, a member of the nobility, and under influence of the intoxication of power, he felt his dignity offended by the peasants claims. It was only through this feeling that, without considering the consequences of what might follow, he sent in a claim to be reinstated in his pretended rights.

SP: And society is held in the thrall of this inequality and intoxication?

LT: Only under the intoxication of the power or the servility of their imagined positions could all these people act as they do. Were they not all firmly convinced that their respective vocations of tsar, minister, governor, judge, nobleman, landowner, superintendent, officer and soldier are something real and important, not one of them would even contemplate – without horror and aversion – doing what they presently do.

Tolstoy pauses for a moment, stroking his beard roughly.

Strange as it may seem, the sole explanation of this astonishing phenomenon is that they are in the condition of the hypnotized, who, they say, feel and act like creatures they are commanded by the hypnotizer to represent.

SP: We play our parts in life as those who are hypnotized? That is a disturbing thought; but makes sense. And leads me now to wonder about the nature of our freedom? If we are hypnotized, can we also be free?

LT: Every man during his life finds himself in regard to truth, in the position of a man walking in the darkness with a light thrown before him by the lantern he carries. He does not see what is not yet lighted up by the lantern; he does not see what he has passed which is hidden in the darkness. But at every stage of his journey, he sees what is lighted up by the lantern; and he can always choose one side or other of the road.

There are always unseen truths as yet unrevealed to the man's intellectual vision; and there are other truths outlived, forgotten, assimilated by him. But there are certain truths with rise up before the light of his reason and require his acknowledgement. And it is in the acknowledgement or non-acknowledgement of these truths that what we call his freedom is manifested. Take the cart horse. A horse harnessed with others to a cart is not free to refrain from moving the cart. If it does not move forward, the cart will knock him down and go on dragging him with it, whether he will it or not. But the horse is free to drag the cart himself or to be dragged with it. And so it is with man.

SP: Not a great freedom.

LT: Well, whether or not this is a great or small degree of freedom in comparison with the fantastic liberty we should like to have, it is the only freedom that really exists; and in it consists the only happiness attainable by man. And more than that, this freedom is the sole means of fulfilling the divine work of the life of the world.

SP: How?

LT: Men need only to comprehend a simple truth; need only to stop troubling themselves about the all the outward ways in which they are not free.

SP: Like the horse.

LT: Instead, they should devote one hundredth part of the energy they waste on those material things, to those areas in which they *are* free. Let them appreciate the truth that is set before them, and commit to freeing themselves and others from deception and hypocrisy. And were it so, without effort or conflict, there would be an immediate end to the false organization of life which makes men miserable, and which threatens them with worse calamities in the future. And then the kingdom of God would be realized! Or at least that first stage of it; for which I believe men are ready now, by the degree of development of their conscience.

SP: But if society as we know it did break down; and something new replaced it: how are we to be sure that what replaces it will be better than what we have?

LT: Hardly any revolution could be more disastrous for the great mass of the population than the present order – or rather disorder – of our life. Consider the daily sacrifices to exhausting and unnatural toil; the poverty, drunkenness and profligacy; and the present horrors of the war, which will swallow up in one year, more victims than all the revolutions of the century.

SIX

Alcohol

In 1885, Tolstoy both gave up alcohol and became a vegetarian, in a bid to make his life simpler. It was a time of letting go, for he also gave up hunting and smoking in this year, and took to wearing peasant uniform, and doing menial tasks. He also believed that people should make their own shoes; though I'm told he didn't make very good ones.

Whether giving up alcohol improved his mood is hard to say. In one of his many rows with his wife Sofya, she actually complained of his non-stop tea drinking. But once he had decided to give up alcohol, the next step, in true Tolstoyan fashion, was to persuade everyone else that he was right. In 1891, Tolstoy attacked alcohol and smoking in Why do Men Stupefy Themselves? *and* God and Mammon, *1895, was a further assault.*

But would he persuade me?

We were walking in fields for most of this conversation. I had borrowed a sun hat from the great man, but carried it after a while, as it was too large; and less appealing for having been soaked over the years in much sweat.

Tolstoy is striding forward and pointing to the horizon as he speaks.

LT: Enormous tracts of the very best lands, by which millions of now poverty-stricken families might be supported, are devoted to tobacco, vineyards, barley, hemp, and especially rye and potatoes to be used in the production of intoxicating beverages: wine, beer and mainly brandy.

SP: And that's a misuse of the land?

LT: Millions of labourers who might be making things useful for men are occupied in the production of these things. In England it is estimated that one-tenth of all the laboring men are occupied in the manufacture of brandy and beer.

SP: Are the consequences so bad? I enjoy a vodka.

LT: There is a terrible story about a monk who laid a wager with the devil that he would not admit him into his cell; if he did let him in, he agreed to do whatever the devil should order him to do. The story tells how the devil took the form of a wounded raven with its bloody wing trailing, and hopped about pitifully at the door of the monk's cell. The monk had compassion for the raven and took him into his cell; and then the devil, having obtained entrance, gave the monk a choice among three crimes: murder, fornication or drunkenness. The monk chose drunkenness, thinking that if he got intoxicated he would harm only himself. But when the liquor had overcome him, he lost control of his reason, went to the village and there, yielding to the temptation of a woman, he committed adultery with her, and then murder, by defending himself from the husband, who returned and attacked him.

Thus are pictured the consequences of drunkenness in the old story, and in no way is it different in real life, for these are the consequences of alcohol. It is an unusual burglar or murderer who perpetrates his crime while sober, for instance. And according to the reports of courts, it is seen that nine-tenths of misdemeanours are committed when people are tipsy.

SP: So you've been gathering evidence.

LT: The most convincing proof that a large number of misdemeanours are traceable to liquor is afforded by the fact that in certain states of America, where wine and the manufacture and sale of intoxicating liquors are prohibited, crimes have almost ceased! There are no robberies, thefts or murders – and the jails are empty!

SP: Slightly hard to believe.

LT: And another consequence is the harmful influence on the health of the people. Besides the fact that from the use of intoxicating drinks arise various painful illnesses peculiar to drunkards, many of whom die of them; it is also to be noted that men who drink alcohol recuperate from ordinary diseases with greater difficulty than others. So that in life insurance, for instance, the insurance companies prefer the risks on those that do not make use of intoxicating drinks.

SP: So health issues are another reason not to drink.

LT: But the third and most horrible consequence of intoxicating beverages is that liquor darkens the intellect and conscience of men; from the use of liquor men grow more coarse, more stupid and yes, more wicked.

SP: So there really are no advantages in alcohol!

LT: None!

SP: Doesn't it improve our mood sometimes?

LT: The gaiety that comes from wine is not real; and not a joyous gaiety. Every one knows what sort of thing this drunken gaiety is. All that it requires is to take a look at what is done in cities on holidays, at the drinking-places, and in the rural districts; at what is done on holidays or at weddings and Christenings. This drunken gaiety always ends with insulting words, fights, injured members, all kinds of crimes and the loss of human dignity.

SP: But there are many good and kind people who do not feel the need to run from alcohol; who can handle it well.

LT: Ah yes, 'Wine,' they say, 'is not to blame, but it's drunkenness which is to be condemned. Christ in Cana of Galilee sanctified wine. If it were not for the drinking habit, then government would be deprived of its chief revenue. And it is impossible to celebrate a holiday, to hold a wedding or a christening without wine! One must drink something at the conclusion of a bargain or a sale; or at a meeting with a dear friend.'

And then the working man says: 'In our poverty and in our labour we must drink.'

And the well-to-do people: 'If we drink only occasionally and temperately, we do no harm to anyone.'

And Prince Vladimir? He says 'The gaiety of Russia is in drinking.'

And we all know what frivolous people say: 'By our drinking we do no harm to any one but ourselves. And if we harm only ourselves then that is our affair; we don't want to teach anyone, and we don't want to be taught by any one; we did not begin this, and it is not for us to put an end to it!'

SP: Yes, I think I've heard all those points of view.

LT: This is how drinking men of various conditions and ages try to justify themselves. But these justifications, which availed some decades of years ago, now no longer avail. It is no longer possible, in our time, to say that the drinking or non-drinking of wine is a private affair. It is impossible to say this now. The use of wine, in our day, is not a private matter, but a public matter.

sp: How so?

lt: We now know what we are doing! And whom we are serving when we use wine and offer it to others! And consequently, if we, who know the sin of using wine, go on drinking or offering it to others, then we have no justification. How – if I know that the use of intoxicating drinks is an evil, destroying hundreds of thousands of men – can I offer this evil to my friends who come to my house for a festival, a christening or a wedding?

sp: Perhaps they'd learn to drink it sensibly at your house.

lt: Drunkards never would have become drunkards if they had not seen honoured men – men respected by every one – drink wine and offer it to others. Do you not see? A young man who has never taken wine will know the taste and the effect of wine at festivals; at weddings; at the houses of these honoured people who are not themselves drunkards, but who drink and set it before their guests on certain occasions.

sp: They are the suppliers.

lt: And so he who drinks wine, no matter how moderately, or offers it in whatever special circumstances, commits a great sin. He tempts those whom he is commanded not to tempt; of whom it is said, 'Woe to him that tempts one of these little ones.'

sp: So your advice is to young and old alike, and always the same.

lt: If you are a young man who have never as yet taken liquor, never as yet been poisoned by the poison of wine – then treasure your innocence and freedom from temptation. If you taste it, the temptation will be all the harder for you to overcome. Oh – and do not believe that wine will increase your gaiety! At your time of life, gaiety is natural, genuine, good gaiety; and wine only changes your true, innocent gaiety into a drunken, senseless, vicious gaiety.

And above all, understand that on you as a man – who have reached the very prime of life, as the master of the house, as the controller of the destiny of others – on you rests the responsibility of guiding the lives of your household. And therefore if you know that wine brings no advantage, but causes great evil to men, then not only are you not obliged slavishly to do as your fathers and grandfathers used to do, to use wine, to buy it and serve it to others; but, on the contrary, you are bound to avoid this habit and keep it from others.

SP: And the attending ridicule from those who don't quite see it your way?

LT: Be not afraid that the change in the custom of drinking wine at festivals, christenings and weddings, will deeply humiliate or trouble people. In many places they have already begun to do this, substituting for the wine appetizing viands and temperance drinks. People at first may wonder about it, but only the most stupid. And quickly, even they get used to it and approve.

SEVEN

India; and the most important thing

Tolstoy has left me in some doubt as to what's coming next. He insists that in this session, we talk about what he calls 'the most important thing'. Perhaps he is teasing me, for he seems to take some pleasure from my uncertainty. But as we sit in his study again, stiff from our morning walk, I first wish to ask about the pressing issue of India.

SP: When asked about western civilization, Gandhi replied that he thought it would be a good idea.

LT: Hah! I've been reading a book about Gandhi. Very important. I must write to him.

I was aware they'd been keeping up a correspondence over the past year; ever since Gandhi wrote to Tolstoy, asking if he might distribute some of his writings on non-violence in South Africa, where he then was. Gandhi had declared himself a great disciple of Tolstoy, particularly appreciating his book, The Kingdom of God is Within You, *which led him to believe that the core of Christianity and Hinduism were one and the same.*

SP: What is your take on British Rule in India?

LT: If the English have enslaved the people of India, it is merely because the latter recognized, and still recognize, force as the fundamental principle of the social order.

SP: So it's the fault of the Indian people themselves?

LT: In accord with the principle of force, they submitted to their little rajahs; and on their behalf, struggled against one another, fought the Europeans, fought the English; and are

Conversations with... Leo Tolstoy

---

now trying to fight with them again. A commercial company enslaved a nation of two hundred million people!

SP: You're referring to the East India Company, which was the first English presence there.

LT: What does it mean that thirty thousand men – not athletes but rather weak and ordinary people – have subdued two hundred million vigorous, clever, capable and freedom-loving people? Do not the figures make it clear that it is not the English who have enslaved the Indians; but the Indians who have enslaved themselves?

SP: They have adopted European ways?

LT: If the people of India are enslaved by violence, it is only because they themselves live and have lived by violence, and do not recognize the eternal law of love inherent in humanity. As soon as men live entirely in accord with the law of love natural to their hearts and now revealed to them, which excludes all resistance by violence; and hold aloof from all participation in violence – well, as soon as this happens, not only will hundreds be unable to enslave millions; but not even millions will be able to enslave a single individual.

SP: They are enslaved by their attitudes.

LT: Do not resist the evil-doer and take no part in doing so, either in the violent deeds of the administration, in the law courts, the collection of taxes, or above all in soldiering – and no one in the world will be able to enslave you.

SP: And Gandhi's point about civilization?

LT: How easy it is for individuals or a country to acquire what is called 'civilization'. You just go to university, keep your nails clean, have a valet or go to the hairdresser, travel abroad and there you have it – you are a civilized person! It is the same for countries: just get more railroads, academies, factories, battleships, fortresses, newspapers, books, political parties, parliaments, and there you have it – a civilized nation. That is why individuals and nations chase after civilization rather than enlightenment. It is easier to do; does not take a lot of effort and everybody approves of it! Whereas pursuing enlightenment takes effort and does not elicit others' approval, but rather their disdain. It is hated by the majority of people, because it exposes the lie of civilization.

SP: Strong words, but we must move on, because I believe you wish to tell me 'the most important thing'.

LT: Indeed.

SP: Well?

LT: There never has been, and cannot be, a good life without self-control.

SP: And that's it?

LT: Apart from self-control, no good life is imaginable. The attainment of goodness must begin with that.

SP: You will need to explain.

LT: Not all men have understood Christianity as an aspiration towards the perfection of the heavenly Father.

SP: For most it is about security on earth, and heaven afterwards.

LT: Precisely. The majority of people have regarded it as a

teaching about salvation; that is, deliverance from sin by grace transmitted through the Church, according to Catholics and Greek Orthodox; by faith in the Redemption, according to Protestants, the Reformed Church, and Calvinists; or, according to some, by means of the two combined.

SP: And this is a bad thing?

LT: It is precisely this teaching that has destroyed the sincerity and seriousness of men's relation to the moral teaching of Christianity. However much the representatives of these faiths may preach that these means of salvation do not hinder man in his aspiration for a good life, but on the contrary contribute toward it – still, from certain assertions, certain deductions necessarily follow. If a man believes that he can be saved through grace transmitted by the Church; or through the sacrifice of the Redemption – well, it is natural for him to think that his own efforts to live a good life are unnecessary, and perhaps even sinful. Consequently, a man who believes that there are means other than personal effort by which he may escape sin or its results, will not strive with the same energy and seriousness, as the man who knows no other means. And this has happened with the majority of those who profess Christianity.

SP: Religion actually allows people to evade the challenge of self-development?

LT: And the same thing happens with those who *cease* to believe in the teaching of the Church. They are like the before-mentioned believers, only they put forward – instead of grace, bestowed by the Church or through Redemption – some imaginary good work, approved of by the majority of men, such as the service of science, art, or humanity. And in the name of this imaginary good work, they liberate themselves from the consecutive attainment of the qualities necessary for a good life; and are satisfied, like men on the stage, with *pretending* to live a good life.

SP: And at the root of it all, 'the most important thing' – is self-control?

LT: In olden times, when there was no Christian teaching, all the teachers of life, beginning with Socrates, regarded self-control as the first virtue of life; and it was understood that every virtue must begin with and pass through this one. It was clear that a man who had no self-control – who had developed an immense number of desires and had yielded himself up to them – could not lead a good life. It was evident that before a man could even think of disinterestedness and justice – to say nothing of generosity or love – he must learn to exercise control over himself. According to our ideas now, however, nothing of the sort is necessary. We are convinced that a man who has many desires, and who cannot live without satisfying the hundred unnecessary habits that enslave him – can somehow still lead an altogether moral and good life.

SP: Could you perhaps give an example?

LT: I have just been reading the letters of one of our highly educated and advanced men of the 'forties, the exile Ogaryóf, written to another yet more highly educated and gifted man, Herzen. In these letters Ogaryóf gives expression to his sincere thoughts and highest aspirations, and one cannot fail to see that – as was natural to a young man – he rather shows off to his friend. He talks of self-perfecting; of sacred friendship, love, the service of science, of humanity, and the like. And yet at the same time, he calmly writes that he often irritates the companion of his life by, as he expresses it, 'returning home in an unsober state, or disappearing for many hours with a fallen, but dear creature. . . .'

SP: Too many desires, all of which must be met?

LT: Evidently it never even occurred to this remarkably kind-hearted, talented, and well-educated man that there was anything at all objectionable in the fact that he, a married man, awaiting the confinement of his wife (in his next letter he writes that his wife has given birth to a child), returned home intoxicated, and disappeared with dissolute women. It did not even enter his head that until he had commenced the struggle, and had, at least to some extent, conquered his inclination to drunkenness and fornication, he could not think of friendship and love – and still less of serving any one or any thing!

SP: No.

LT: But here's the wonder – not only did he not struggle against these vices; he evidently thought there was something very nice in them, and that they did not in the least hinder the struggle for perfection! And so instead of hiding them from the friend, in whose eyes he wishes to appear in a good light – he actually exhibits them!

SP: I see your point.

LT: The delusion that men while addicting themselves to their desires – and regarding this life of desire as good – can yet lead a good, useful, just and loving life, is so astonishing, that I think men of later generations will simply fail to understand what the men of our time meant by the words 'good life' – when they said that the gluttons – the effeminate, lustful sluggards – of our wealthy classes, led good lives. Men of the wealthy classes have no right even to *talk* about a good life.

SP: And what is a good life?

LT: The less a man loves himself, the easier it becomes for him to be better; and contrariwise.

SP: And how do we do that? How do we love ourselves less?

LT: In order to love others in reality and not only in word, one must cease to love one's self also in reality, and not merely in word. In most cases it happens thus: we think we love others, and we assure ourselves and others that it is so; but we love them only in words, while ourselves, we love in reality. Others we forget to feed and put to bed, but ourselves – never! Therefore, in order really to love others in deed, we must learn not to love ourselves in deed; learn to forget to feed ourselves and put ourselves to bed – exactly as we forget to do these things for others.

SP: And that's self-control.

LT: There is a scale of virtues, and it is necessary, if one would mount the higher steps, to begin with the lowest; and the first virtue a man must acquire if he wishes to acquire the others, is that which the ancients called *enkrateia*— that is, self-control or moderation. And the effort towards self-control commences with a struggle against the lust of gluttony; commences with fasting.

SP: So it all starts with our attitude to food?

LT: Just as the first condition of a good life is self-control, so the first condition of a life of self-control, is fasting.

SP: But why is our attitude towards food so important? I'm struggling to see quite why you elevate it in this way.

LT: From the poorest to the richest, eating is, I think, the chief aim, the chief pleasure, of our life. Poor working people form an exception, but only inasmuch as want prevents their addicting themselves to this passion. No sooner have they the time and the means, than, in imitation of the higher classes, they procure what is most tasty and sweet; and eat and drink as much as they can. And the more they eat, the more do they deem themselves not only happy, but also strong and healthy! And they are encouraged in this conviction, of course, by the upper classes, who regard food in precisely the same way. The educated classes – following the medical men who assure them that the most expensive food – flesh – is the most wholesome, imagine that happiness and health consist in tasty, nourishing, easily digested food and in gorging; though they try to conceal this.

SP: I'm not sure everyone is quite as obsessed with food as you imagine.

LT: Look at rich people's lives, listen to their conversation! What lofty subjects seem to occupy them: philosophy; science; art; poetry; the distribution of wealth; the welfare of the people and the education of the young. But all this is, for the immense majority, a sham; for all this occupies them in the intervals of business, the *real* business: between lunch and dinner, while the stomach is full and it is impossible to eat more. The only real living interest of the majority both of men and women, especially after early youth, is eating: how to eat, what to eat, where and when to eat?

SP: You think?

LT: No solemnity, no rejoicing, no consecration, no opening of anything, can dispense with eating. Or watch people travelling. In their case, the thing is especially evident. 'Museums, libraries, Parliament – how very interesting! But where shall we dine? Where is one best fed?' Or look at people when they come together for dinner, dressed up, perfumed, around a table decorated with flowers – how joyfully they rub their hands and smile!

Oh yes, if we could look into the hearts of the majority of people, what should we find they most desire? Appetite for breakfast and for dinner. What is the severest punishment from infancy upwards? To be put on bread and water. What artisans get the highest wages? Cooks. What is the chief interest of the mistress of the house? To what subject does the conversation of middle-class housewives generally tend? If the conversation of the members of the higher classes does not tend in the same direction, it is not because they are better educated or are occupied with higher interests, but simply because they have a house-keeper or a steward who relieves them of all anxiety about their dinner. But once deprive them of this convenience, and you will see what causes them most anxiety. It all comes round to the subject of eating: the price of grouse, the best way of making coffee, of baking sweet cakes, things like this.

SP: People need to eat.

LT: The satisfaction of a need has limits; but pleasure has none. For the satisfaction of our needs, it is necessary and sufficient to eat bread, porridge, or rice; for the augmentation of pleasure there is no end to the possible flavourings and seasonings. Believe me, one may wish to be good; one may dream of goodness, without fasting; but to be good without fasting is as impossible as it is to advance without getting up on to one's feet.

EIGHT

Vegetarianism

Tolstoy is supposed to have been converted to the vegetarian cause by a single conversation with William Frey, one afternoon in 1885. Frey had spoken of the inevitability of vegetarianism and the naturalness of such a diet. Tolstoy had thought for a moment, and then declared: 'Yes, my friend, you are quite right. Thanks, thanks for your wise and honest words! I will certainly follow your example and abandon flesh-meat.'

And concerning this matter, a rather embarrassing incident occurred on the second evening of my stay; cruel comedy to make a point.

It was dinner time at Yasnaya Polyana. Tolstoy's aunt came to the table to find a carving knife and a live chicken on her chair. Those of us there, watched uncomfortably. Unsurprisingly, the woman was much disturbed at this discovery and started to complain loudly. Sofya was also angry. And then I remember Tolstoy saying to his aunt something like: 'We knew you wanted chicken, but none of us would kill it!'

Two of his children had followed him into vegetarianism, but not his wife or his aunt, and he did not sit comfortably with this. He liked people to agree with him. It was me, however, whom he cornered after the meal, as I loitered in the hall. He asked if I had ever been to an abattoir. Before I could answer, he was telling me of his visit.

LT: Through the door opposite the one at which I was standing, a big, red, well-fed ox was led in. Two men were dragging it, and hardly had it entered when I saw a butcher raise a knife above its neck and stab it. The ox, as if all four legs had suddenly given way, fell heavily upon its belly, immediately turned over on one side, and began to work its legs and all its hindquarters. Another butcher at once threw himself upon the ox from the side opposite to the twitching legs, caught its horns and twisted its head down to the ground, while another butcher cut its throat with a knife. From beneath the head there flowed a stream of blackish-red blood, which a besmeared boy caught in a tin basin. All the time this was going on, the ox kept incessantly twitching its head as if trying to get up, and waved its four legs in the air. The basin was quickly filling, but the ox still lived, and, its stomach heaving heavily, both hind and fore legs worked so violently that the butchers held aloof. When one basin was full, the boy carried it away on his head to the albumen factory, while another boy placed a fresh basin, which also soon began to fill up. But still the ox heaved its body and worked its hind legs.

SP: You speak as though you're still there watching.

LT: When the blood ceased to flow the butcher raised the animal's head and began to skin it. The ox continued to writhe. The head, stripped of its skin, showed red with white veins, and kept the position given it by the butcher; on both sides hung the skin. Still the animal did not cease to writhe. Then another butcher caught hold of one of the legs, broke it, and cut it off. In the remaining legs and the stomach the convulsions still continued. The other legs were cut off and thrown aside, together with those of other oxen belonging to the same owner. Then the carcass was dragged to the hoist and hung up, and the convulsions were over.

I stood there in the hallway in silence; what was there to say?

LT: This is dreadful.

SP: It is dreadful.

LT: Not the suffering and the death of the animals, but that people can suppress in themselves, unnecessarily, the highest spiritual capacity.

SP: Which is?

LT: Sympathy and pity towards fellow creatures like themselves; and by violating their own feelings, become cruel.

SP: You're saying that the killer suffers as much trauma as the killed; that in the act of killing, something in them dies, and they become hardened; brutalized.

LT: And of course, how deeply seated in the human heart is the injunction not to take life. The commandment 'You shall not kill' does not apply to murder of one's own kind only; but to all living beings.

SP: So are you saying then that all moral people must cease to eat meat?

LT: Not at all.

SP: It does sound as though you are.

LT: I only wish to say that for a good life, a certain order of good actions is indispensable; that if a man's aspirations toward right living be serious, they will inevitably follow one definite sequence ; and that in this sequence, the first virtue a man will strive after will be self-control, self-restraint.

SP: We've talked about this.

LT: And now we talk about it again, for in seeking self-control, a man will inevitably follow one definite sequence, and in this sequence the first thing will be self-control in food

– fasting. And in fasting, if he is really and seriously seeking to live a good life, the first thing from which he will abstain will always be the use of animal food, because – quite apart from the stimulation of the passions caused by such food – its use is simply immoral. Meat-eating involves the performance of an act which is contrary to the moral feeling; that is, killing. And it arises from nothing more worthy than greediness and the desire for tasty food.

Tolstoy then disappeared into his study, closing the door behind him.

NINE

When the stupid rule

Tolstoy had been a hero in organizing famine relief in the Samsara district, in 1891, and attacked the government response to the famine. As for the government, they simply viewed him as a socialist, an anarchist and a liberalizing revolutionary.

In reality, Tolstoy had never advocated revolutionary violence. Neither, however, would he enter into any sort of dialogue with the government. Rather, he chose unending hostility though words. Tolstoy didn't discuss; he declared.

The early morning sunlight shines into his study, as we settle down again.

SP: So tell me: are you angrier with those in power – or with the oppressed who allow them to remain there?

LT: The crowd are so hypnotized that although they see what is going on, they do not understand its meaning. They see what constant care Kings, Emperors and Presidents devote to their disciplined armies; they see the reviews, parades and manoeuvres the rulers hold, about which they boast to one another. And the people crowd to see their own brothers, brightly dressed up in fools' clothes, turned into machines to the sound of drum and trumpet; all, at the shout of one man, making one and the same movement at one and the same moment! But they do not understand what it all means.

SP: And what does it all mean?

LT: The meaning of this drilling is very clear and simple: it is nothing but a preparation for killing. It is stupefying men in order to make them fit instruments for murder.

SP: Which all governments take part in, surely?

LT: Of course. One only need remember that similar oppression and similar war went on, no matter who was at the head of the Government – Nicholas or Alexander, Frederick or Wilhelm, Napoleon or Louis, Palmerston or Gladstone, McKinley or anyone else – in order to understand that it is not any particular person who causes these oppressions and these wars from which the nations suffer.

SP: So what is the source of the misery?

LT: The misery of nations is caused not by particular persons, but by the particular social order under which the people are so tied up together, that they find themselves all in the power of a few men; or more often, in the power of one single man: a man so perverted by his unnatural position as arbiter of the fate and lives of millions, that he is always in an unhealthy state, and always suffers more or less from a mania of self-aggrandizement, which only his exceptional position conceals from general notice.

SP: Can you be more specific about this 'unhealthy state' of our leaders?

LT: Apart from the fact that such men are surrounded from earliest childhood to the grave by the most insensate luxury; and that an atmosphere of falsehood and flattery accompanies them throughout this time – their whole education and all their occupations are centred on one object: learning about former murders, the best present-day ways of murdering, and the best preparations for future murder.

SP: I can see it's not the most enlightened education.

LT: From childhood, they learn about killing in all its possible forms. They always carry about with them murderous weapons – swords or sabres; they dress themselves in various uniforms; they attend parades, reviews and manoeuvres; they visit one another, and present one another with Orders and nominating one another to the command of regiments! And remarkably, not only does no one tell them plainly what they are doing; or say that to busy one's self with preparations for killing is revolting and criminal – but from all sides they hear nothing but approval and enthusiasm for all this activity of theirs! Every time they go out, and at each parade and review, crowds of people flock to greet them with enthusiasm, and it seems to them as if the whole nation approves of their conduct.

SP: There's always the press to expose them. Or at least ask questions.

LT: The only part of the Press which they see, and which they take be the expression of the feelings of the whole people – or at least of its best representatives – slavishly extols their every word and deed, however silly or wicked they may be. Those around them, men and women, clergy and laity – all people who do not prize human dignity – vie with one another in refined flattery, agree with them about anything, and deceive them about everything, making it impossible for them to see life as it is. I tell you, such rulers might live a hundred years without ever seeing one single really independent person; or ever hearing the truth spoken.

SP: The powerful are surrounded by flunkeys; yes-men.

LT: One is sometimes appalled to hear of the words and deeds of these men; but one need only consider their position in order to understand that anyone in their place would act as they do.

SP: Given the setting and expectations, I suppose it would be foolish of the courtiers to act in any other way.

LT: If any reasonable man found himself in their place, there is only one reasonable action he could perform, and that would be to get away from such a position. Any one remaining in it would behave as they do.

SP: There is a madness to it all.

LT: What, indeed, must go on in the head of Wilhelm of Germany – a narrow-minded, ill-educated, vain man, with the ideals of a German Junker – when there is nothing he can say so stupid or so horrid that it will not be met by an enthusiastic 'Hoch!'; and be commented on by the Press of the entire world as though it were something highly important?

SP: Do we laugh or do we cry?

LT: When he says that, at his word, soldiers should be ready to kill their own fathers, people shout 'Hurrah!' When he says that the Gospel must be introduced with an iron fist, again – 'Hurrah!' When he says the army is to take no prisoners in China, but to slaughter everybody – no, he is not put into a lunatic asylum, but people shout 'Hurrah!' and set sail for China to execute his commands! Or Nicholas II – a man naturally modest – begins his reign by announcing to venerable old men –

SP: – The Decembrists –

LT: – who had expressed a wish to be allowed to discuss their own affairs, that such ideas of self-government were 'insensate dreams.' And what does the Press say? And what do those he meets say? They praise him for it. He proposes a childish, silly and hypocritical project of universal peace, while at the same time ordering an increase in the army – and there are no limits to the laudations of his wisdom and virtue. Without any need, he foolishly and mercilessly insults and oppresses a whole nation, the Finns; and again, he hears nothing but praise. Finally, he arranges the Chinese slaughter – terrible in its injustice, cruelty and incompatibility with his peace projects – and from all sides, people applaud him, both as a victor and as a continuer of his father's peace policy. What must be going on in the heads and hearts of these men?

SP: So what needs to happen in the face of stupid rule? Some favour political assassination. But you regard assassination as not only immoral, but a waste of time.

LT: That nations should not be oppressed, and that there should be none of these useless wars; and that men may not be indignant with those who seem to cause these evils, and may not kill them – it seems that only a very small thing is necessary.

SP: Which is?

LT: It is necessary that men should understand things as they are. We must call them by their right names, and should know that an army is an instrument for killing, and that the enrolment and management of an army – the very things which Kings, Emperors and Presidents occupy themselves with so self-confidently – is a preparation for murder.

SP: Things are not generally named in such a way.

LT: If only each King, Emperor and President understood that his work of directing armies is not an honourable and important duty, as his flatterers persuade him it is; but rather, a bad and shameful act of preparation for murder! And if each private individual understood that the payment of taxes through which soldiers are hired and equipped, and, above all, army-service itself – that these are not matters of indifference, but are bad and shameful actions by which he himself not only permits but participates in murder – then this power of Emperors, Kings and Presidents, which now arouses our indignation, and which causes them to be assassinated, would disappear of itself.

SP: But people do not see things this way; nor act in this way.

LT: If people do not yet act in this way, it is only because Governments, to maintain themselves, diligently exercise a hypnotic influence upon the people. And, therefore, we may help to prevent people killing either Kings or one another, not by killing – murder only increases the hypnotism – but by arousing people from their hypnotic condition. And it is this I have always tried to do.

TEN
Personal matters

It is not possible to spend time at Yasnaya Polyana, without becoming aware of the tensions in the home. I had heard gossip that Tolstoy's marriage was an increasing nightmare; and nothing which I have witnessed contradicts this.

It was not always so, of course. In the early days, Sofya Bers had been a close partner in her husband's success. Tolstoy himself acknowledged her as his literary assistant, publicist and manager.

They had married in 1862 and had 13 children together. And it was Sofya who had diligently copied out his writings, prepared them for publication, and frequently dealt with the publishers. She was fifteen years younger than Tolstoy, and before their marriage, Tolstoy gave her a diary detailing his extensive sexual exploits, believing married people should have no secrets.

But two factors caused estrangement. First, increasingly, they didn't share the same aspirations. Sofya was not impressed with Leo's new 'spiritual' self, with all its rules of behaviour. She did not follow him into vegetarianism, which frustrated Tolstoy, and he often thought of divorce. For him, she was not serious-minded enough; too concerned with furniture, servants, society and the education of their children.

Second, Chertkov was now the significant figure for Tolstoy. We need not go into the whole story here, but by the time I visited the household, Chertkov – Tolstoy's keenest disciple – was clearly seen as a threat by Sofya, and with good reason. On his return from exile last year, he had built a house 3 miles from Yasnaya; and was increasingly involved in battles with Sofya over ownership of Tolstoy's manuscripts and diaries. He was now Tolstoy's closest companion, and doing all that Sofya used to do. Sofya did not trust their scheming.

By the end, it appeared Tolstoy loved Chertkov almost as much as he hated his wife. He now sought ideological friends; friends who agreed with him, and Chertkov was said to be more Tolstoyan than Tolstoy. Increasingly, Tolstoy could not have a relationship with someone with whom he disagreed. And that was most people!

Before arriving, I had read a novella which Tolstoy wrote in 1859. It was called Family Happiness, *and was written when he was contemplating marriage. It was an attempt by Tolstoy to understand how married life might work for a man now in his early thirties, and experienced in the ways of the world. In the story, Masha, the young female protagonist, marries Sergey, a much older and more worldly man. Sergey, aware of the age difference, tries to raise his wife to be a responsible woman. Masha, in turn, discovers their marriage is not the bliss she imagined. Finally, the most they can hope for is peace and compatibility.*

However, even this seemed a dream too far for Leo and Sofya. On one afternoon, Sofya told me that her unhappiness had left her 'unhinged'. She often threatened suicide, whether by morphine or drowning, and didn't sleep a lot. There were times of calm, though; a housemaid told me they got on best when Tolstoy was ill and she was able to care for him.

In the meantime, Tolstoy had insisted I help clear some land on the south side of the estate. He seemed happy with the scythe in his hand; and in between assaults on the weeds, he was surprisingly candid about himself – almost insisting on self-revelation.

LT: I suffer, you know, because my wife does not share my convictions. But when I speak with her in fear of her rebuffing me, I often speak coldly; even in an unfriendly manner.

SP: You are unhappy with the way you have behaved towards her?

LT: I have entreated her with tears to believe in the truth; but I've never expressed all my thoughts to her in a loving and gentle fashion. There she is lying beside me, and I say nothing to her! And what I ought to, what I ought to say to her, I say to God.

I leave a silence.

SP: So you blame yourself; do you also blame her?

LT: Maybe. She lacks the habit of, even the strength for, a spiritual life.

SP: How so?

LT: All her strength has been expended on her children who are no longer here.

With talk of children – which I note he refers to as 'hers' – I seize the moment, and ask Tolstoy about his attitudes to sex. After much sexual activity in his youth, he was famous now for being a puritan in these matters. Even by the time he was finishing Anna Karenina, *he frowned on sexual intercourse for any other purpose than the procreation of children; and reiterated this stance in his essay* What Then Must We Do?

SP: Sex is one of many topics which seems to disturb you.

LT: I do know for certain that copulation is an abomination which can only be thought of with revulsion, under the influence of sexual desire.

SP: You mean that only desire makes possible the pursuit of

such an indecent act?

LT: Even in order to have children, you wouldn't do this to a woman you love. And I say this at a time when I'm myself possessed by sexual desire, against which I can't fight. I am a dirty, libidinous old man.

SP: Does that depress you?

LT: Generally, my state of mind is one of dissatisfaction with myself – but not depression.

SP: Is it possible to make that distinction?

LT: No. I am in a terrible depression at my disgusting life in contrast to the hard lives of the working people around me who are trying to keep themselves and their families from dying of cold and hunger.

SP: But you do what you can.

LT: Huh! At my table yesterday, fifteen people were stuffing themselves with pancakes, while five or six servants were running around barely able to prepare and serve the food. It is unbearably shameful and terrible. And also yesterday – in the afternoon – I rode past some road workers who were breaking rocks, and I felt like I was running a gauntlet. Their poverty and envy and hatred of the rich is depressing; but my shameful lifestyle is even more depressing.

After further hard labour in the fields, we are returning to the house, covered in sweat. And one final question occurs to me, in what has been a revealing time together:

SP: So how have you changed down the years, sir?

LT: How have I changed? In my youth I was worried about bad things happening to me, and I wanted what was best only for me and for the health of my organism. In my old age, I worry about bad things happening to everyone else, and I desire our common good, and the good of the common organism. May God help me orient myself in such a way that 'I' disappear and only God passes through me.

ELEVEN

The self-indulgent rich

Count Leo Tolstoy was a privileged man in two ways. Not only was he born into a well-known family of Russian nobility, connected to the grandest Russian aristocracy. He had also made a personal fortune from his writing.

Yet despite his own privileged setting, he is scathing against the rich, and I wish to ask him about this. His rage against privilege echoes with his rage at himself. I wonder if it is a form of self-purgation.

SP: You are rich. But you do not like the rich.

LT: A man accustomed to the life of our well-to-do classes cannot lead a righteous life without first coming out of those conditions of evil in which he is immersed; he cannot begin to do good until he has ceased to do evil. It is impossible for a man living in luxury to lead a righteous life.

SP: But the wealthy know of the inequality?

LT: These people know that the distribution of pleasures among men is unequal, and regard this inequality as an evil, and wish to correct it, yes. Yet they do not cease to strive to augment their own pleasures; that is, to augment inequality in the distribution of pleasures.

SP: They want change as long as it doesn't involve them?

LT: These people are like men who being the first to enter an orchard hasten to gather all the fruit they can lay their hands on; and yet also wish to organize a more equal distribution of the fruit of the orchard between themselves and later comers

– while they continue to pluck all the fruit they can reach! A self-indulgent man who sleeps long upon a soft bed; eats and drinks abundance of fat, sweet food; who is always dressed cleanly and suitably to the temperature; and who has never accustomed himself to the effort of laborious work, can in fact do very little.

SP: For those of us who don't know, you must tell us about the life of the rich.

LT: A person, man or woman, sleeps on a spring-bed with two mattresses, and two smooth, clean sheets, and feather pillows in pillow cases. By the bedside is a rug, so that their feet don't get cold on stepping out of bed; though slippers also lie near. Here also are the necessary utensils, so that he need not leave the house; whatever uncleanliness he may produce will be carried away, and all made tidy. The windows are covered with curtains that the daylight may not awaken him, and he sleeps as long as he is inclined. Besides all this, measures are taken that the room may be warm in winter and cool in summer; and that he may not be disturbed by the noise of flies or other insects, while he sleeps; water, hot and cold, for his ablutions – and sometimes baths and preparations for shaving – are provided. Tea and coffee are also prepared, stimulating drinks to be taken immediately upon rising. Boots, shoes, galoshes – several pairs dirtied the previous day – are already being cleaned and made to shine like glass, freed from every speck of dust. Similarly are cleaned various garments, soiled on the preceding day, differing in texture to suit not only summer and winter, but also spring, autumn, rainy, damp and warm weather. Clean linen – washed, starched, and ironed – is being made ready with studs, shirt buttons, and buttonholes, all carefully inspected by specially appointed people.

SP: So what time do they get up in the morning?

The self-indulgent rich

LT: If the person be active, he rises early – at seven o'clock – i.e., still a couple of hours later than those who are making all these preparations for him. Besides clothes for the day and covering for the night, there is also costume and foot-gear for the time of dressing – dressing-gown and slippers; and now he undertakes his washing, cleaning and brushing, for which several kinds of brushes are used, as well as soap and a great quantity of water. Many English men and women, for some reason or other, are specially proud of using a great deal of soap and pouring a large quantity of water over themselves.

SP: The rush to be cleaner-than-thou.

LT: Then he dresses, brushes his hair before a special kind of looking-glass – different from those that hang in almost every room in the house – takes the things he needs, such as spectacles or eyeglasses, and then distributes in different pockets a clean pocket-handkerchief to blow his nose on; a watch with a chain, though in almost every room he goes to there will be a clock; money of various kinds, small change (often in a specially contrived case which saves him the trouble of looking for the required coin) and bank-notes. He also takes visiting cards on which his name is printed, saving him the trouble of saying or writing it; oh, and pocket-book and pencil. In the case of women, the toilet is still more complicated: corsets, arranging of long hair, adornments, laces, elastics, ribbons, ties, hairpins, pins and brooches.

SP: Yes, I can see it all takes a while.

LT: But at last all is complete and the day commences, generally with eating: tea and coffee are drunk with a great quantity of sugar; bread made of the finest white flour is eaten with large quantities of butter, and sometimes the flesh of pigs. The men, for the most part, smoke cigars or cigarettes, and read fresh papers, which have just been brought. Then, leaving to others the task of setting right the soiled and disordered room, they go to their office or business; or perhaps drive in carriages produced specially to move such people about. Then comes a luncheon of slain beasts, birds and fish, followed by a dinner consisting, if it be very modest, of three courses, dessert and coffee. After this, they play at cards and play music – or the theatre, reading and conversation in soft spring armchairs, by the intensified and shaded light of candles, gas or electricity. After this, more tea, more eating – supper – and then to bed – a bed shaken up and prepared with clean linen; and with washed utensils to be made foul again soon.

Thus pass the days of a man of modest life, of whom, if he is good-natured and does not possess any habits specially obnoxious to those about him, it is said that he leads a good and virtuous life!

SP: I'm sure you could write a wicked story about all this.

LT: I have long wished to write a fairy-tale of this kind : A woman, wishing to revenge herself on one who has injured her, carries off her enemy's child, and, going to a sorcerer, asks him to teach her how she can most cruelly wreak her vengeance on the stolen infant, the only child of her enemy. The sorcerer bids her carry the child to a place he indicates, and assures her that a most terrible vengeance will result. The wicked woman follows his advice; but, keeping an eye upon the child, is astonished to see that it is found and adopted by a wealthy, childless man. She goes to the sorcerer and reproaches him, but he bids her wait. The child grows up in luxury and effeminacy. The woman is perplexed, but again the sorcerer bids her wait. And at length, the time comes when the wicked woman is not only satisfied, but has even to pity her victim. He grows up in the effeminacy and dissoluteness of wealth; and owing to his good nature is ruined. Then begins a sequence of physical sufferings, poverty, and humiliation, to which he is especially sensitive and against which he knows not how to contend. I can see it all. The weakness of his effeminate body accustomed to luxury and idleness; vain struggles; lower and still lower decline; drunkenness to drown thought, and then finally crime and insanity – or suicide.

SP: There's nothing like a happy ending; and this is nothing like a happy ending!

LT: I cannot but repeat this same thing again and again, notwithstanding the cold and hostile silence with which my words are received.

TWELVE
God?

I suppose A Confession *has been Tolstoy's pivotal philosophical writing since his period of spiritual change, detailing as it does, his life's search for religious truth and for God.*

'Man discovers truth by reason only; not by faith,' he says – so in many ways, Tolstoy remains the supreme rationalist. I am, therefore, interested to see where a divine being fits into all this, as we sit in his study after our evening meal.

He may have been excommunicated by the Church; but as I discover, he has much to say about God.

SP: You feel religion has distorted our picture of God?

LT: Religion is the definition of one's relationship with the world, and determines all our actions. Usually, however, people establish their relationship with the source of everything – God – and then to that same God, they attribute their own characteristics of punishing, rewarding, wanting to receive respect and love – which in essence, are only human qualities. We invent our own human-like God and relate to him as if he were like us, attributing our characteristics to him. This is anthropomorphism, which more than anything else, diminishes God and distorts our religious understanding. Indeed, every endeavour of the imagination to know Him more definitely (for instance, as my Creator, or as a Merciful Being) removes me farther from Him, and prevents me drawing nearer to Him.

SP: So we shouldn't domesticate God?

LT: He is necessarily such that I cannot comprehend or name

Him. If I understood Him, I should have reached Him, and there would be nothing to strive after and there would be no life. But, and this seems a contradiction, though I cannot understand or name Him – yet at the same time I know Him and the direction toward Him.

SP: A bold claim.

LT: Of all the things I know, this is the most certain. For me He is the Father of what I call the highest in me. Of course, He requires that my life should be the realization of what is highest in the flesh, of what He produces in me.

SP: And I know consciousness is important for you.

LT: Life in me is consciousness. Consciousness is not mine, in that it does not depend on my will – it comes and goes as it wishes. But when it is in me, then I am not less than it.

SP: Explain.

LT: I am perfectly conscious of my consciousness; it is the most unquestionable of all things that exist. Consciousness has no time or space; it has nothing personal, and is neither good nor evil. I am alive while I am conscious, and when it is in me; I cannot be unconscious of it. This consciousness is also God. I cannot know what God is outside of me; and though I cannot know when consciousness will arise in me, I do know it when it does. I also know that I and consciousness are not one, but two things.

SP: How do you know that?

LT: Because consciousness may be for me a pain and a happiness, according as I treat it.

SP: So consciousness is a moral force which people can rebel against?

LT: If a man rebels against consciousness, then for him immediately and forever the present perishes, and he is in death; in other words, he is deprived of consciousness, and this death is absolute, without the slightest relief, since this death from a quarrel with consciousness means deprivation of all life. If a man, however, serves consciousness with his reason, then he is in complete life, and for him there is no trace of death, nothing terrible and unknown; this man is then endlessly alive, as alive as consciousness itself.

SP: So do you know God purely through reason?

LT: One knows God, not so much through reason, nor even through the heart; but through one's feeling of complete dependence on Him. It is akin to the feeling experienced by a baby in the arms of its mother. It does not know who holds it, warms it, feeds it; but it does know that there is this someone; and more than merely knows it, loves that being.

And really, it is astonishing how I could formerly fail to see this indubitable truth; see that behind this world and our life in it, there is some one or something that knows why this world exists, and why we in it, like bubbles in boiling water, rise, burst and then disappear.

SP: And so your religion is no leap of faith – but makes sense.

LT: All that I know, I know because there is a God, and because I know Him. Only upon this can one firmly base one's relations with other men and with oneself, as well as with life outside space and time. Not only do I not regard this as mystical; but I believe the opposite view to be mystical. My way is the most intelligible and accessible reality.

God?

SP: Yet for all this talk, you do not acknowledge God a great deal in your writings.

LT: You say that I do not seem to acknowledge God? This is a misunderstanding. I acknowledge nothing but God. God is that *un*limited *all* which I know within myself in a limited form. I am limited, God is infinite; I am a being which has lived eighty one years, God lives eternally; I am a being which reasons within the limits of its understanding, God reasons without limit; I am a being which loves sometimes a little, God loves always infinitely. I am a part, He is all. I cannot understand myself, other than as a part of Him.

SP: You are part of the divine body?

LT: Indeed. When an unsolved question torments one, then one feels oneself to be a diseased member of some whole, healthy body; one feels oneself to be an unsound tooth in a sound body, and asks the whole body to help the one member. The whole body is God; the member is myself.

SP: So do you think about God all the time?

LT: The consciousness or the sensation of God who is living in me and acting through me, cannot be felt always. Clearly there are activities to which one has got to give oneself up altogether, unlimitedly, without thinking of anything save that one thing. In these cases, it is impossible to think of God; it would distract, and is unnecessary.

SP: So when is the right time to think of God?

LT: One should live simply, without exertion, giving oneself up to one's tendencies; but the moment there arises inward doubt, struggle, despondency, fear or ill-will, then immediately – recognizing in oneself one's spiritual being, recognizing one's connection with God – one should transport oneself from the material into the spiritual region; and that not in order to escape the work of life, but, on the contrary, to gather strength for its accomplishment, for the victory over, the mastering of, the obstacle. We should be like the bird. We advance on our legs with folded wings; but the moment an obstacle is encountered, then we unfold our wings and fly up, and find relief as our burden disappears.

SP: Some people – like St. Paul on the Damascus Road – experience a definite conversion experience.

LT: This is what has happened to me: I began to think more and more abstractedly about the problems of life. In what does life consist? What is its aim? What is love? And I got farther and farther away, not only from the Old Testament conception of God the Creator, but also from the conception of Him as a Father, the righteous source of all life, and of my own being. And the devil ensnared me, and it began to enter my mind that it is possible, for the sake of good relations with the Chinese Confucians, and with the Buddhists and our own atheists and agnostics, altogether to avoid this conception. I thought it was possible to restrict oneself to the conception and acknowledgment of that God only which is in me, without acknowledging any God apart from that; without acknowledging the One who has implanted in me a particle of Himself. And, strange to say, I suddenly began to feel dull, depressed and alarmed. I did not know the cause of this, but I felt that I had suddenly undergone a dreadful spiritual fall; had lost all spiritual joy and energy.

SP: And then?

LT: And then only did I comprehend that this had happened because I had deserted God, and in doing so, I found Him, as it were, afresh! And I was filled with such joy, and such a firm assurance did I gain of Him; and of the possibility and duty of communion with Him, and of His hearing me. And my joy grew so great that all these last days, I have been experiencing the feeling that something very good has come to me, and I keep asking myself, 'Why do I feel so happy? Yes! God! There is a God, and I need be neither anxious nor afraid, but can only rejoice.'

SP: Wonderful.

LT: All that I might write would not express what I have felt. Whether I am suffering physical or moral pain, whether my son is dying, or that which I love is perishing and I cannot help it, or sufferings are awaiting me, suddenly the thought recurs to me: 'And how about God?' and all becomes good and joyous and clear. Indeed, I live only at those times I believe in God. I need only to be aware of God to live. I need only forget him or disbelieve him, and I die. 'Live seeking God', an inner voice told me, and then you will not live without God.

SP: These are intense feelings.

LT: I am afraid that this feeling will pass away, will grow dull; but for the present it is very joyous. It is as if I had been within a hair's-breadth of losing – no, thought that I had actually lost – the Being dearest to me; and yet had not so lost Him, but had only realized His priceless worth. I hope, if it does pass away, that it will only be the ecstatic feeling; and that there will remain much of what I have newly gained. Perhaps this is what some call the 'living God'; if that be so, then I did very wrong toward them in contradicting them, instead of agreeing with them.

SP: And what's the best thing about all this?

LT: The chief thing in this feeling is a consciousness of entire security, a consciousness that He is, that He is good, that He knows me, and that I am entirely surrounded by Him, that I have come from Him, and am going to Him, form a part of Him, am His child. All that seems bad, seems so only because I trust to myself and not in Him

SP: And do you ever experience doubt now?

LT: There is not one believing man to whom moments of doubt do not come; doubt in the existence of God. And these doubts are not harmful; on the contrary, they lead to a higher understanding of God. God becomes too familiar, and we entirely believe in God only when He discloses Himself afresh to us.

SP: And can we aid that process?

LT: He discloses Himself to us in a fresh way when we seek Him with all our soul. One should never go to God casually. 'Now let me just go to God; and I will begin to live according to God. Why not? I have been living according to the devil, but let me now try to live according to God. Who knows – perhaps no harm will come of it?'

SP: This is not a good attitude?

LT: There is harm in this, and great harm. Coming to God is something like getting married: one should do it only when one would be glad not to come to Him – or not to get married – but cannot help doing so.

SP: We must be desperate for God rather than calculating in our approach?

LT: It is not that I would tell a man: 'Go purposely into temptations.' But to the one who weighs up the advantages and disadvantages of going to God rather than the devil, I would cry out as loud as I can: 'Go, go to the devil, by all means to the devil!' It is a hundred times better to get well scalded against the devil, than to continually stand at the cross-roads, or insincerely go to God.

SP: But hasn't Darwin changed the way we talk about God forever; or indeed disproved God?

LT: Not at all. Nothing better proves the existence of God than the attempts of the evolutionists to accept morality and deduce it from the struggle for existence. It is obvious that morality cannot emanate from struggle. Saying that the world arose due to evolution or due to God having created it in six days are both equally stupid. The only smart thing is to admit that I do not know how it originated and I cannot know it and it is not necessary for me to know it.

SP: So for you, God exists. But can religion exist?

LT: In everything we do, it is important to stop at the point we do not know something; and not think we know something when we do not. This sort of restraint is most vital in the area of religion and belief. All nonsensical religious superstitions result only from this lack of restraint. Rather, in establishing one's religion, it is best to leave God in peace and refrain from ascribing to Him not only the creation of paradise and hell, anger, the desire to atone for sins and other such nonsense; but also to refrain from attributing to him will, desire and even love. Leave God in peace, and understand him to be completely beyond our comprehension, and instead, base your religion and your relationship to the world on the traits of rationality and love, which are intrinsic to us. This will be a religion of truth and love – like all the other religions in the true sense of the word, from the Brahmins to Christ; but it will be even more clear, correct and compelling.

In my room that evening, with the household quiet, I reflect on Tolstoy's request that we leave God in peace; and I wonder if that is what his father said to him: 'Leave me in peace!' Leo Tolstoy does seem to have created a God in his father's image – a distant figure, and often away; yet also the key parent with the death of his mother; warm on occasion, and the one on whom he was utterly dependent. Sometimes Tolstoy seems happy for God to be described as loving. At other times, it is not deemed an appropriate description. And nor should such love be demanded, he tells me – as no doubt the little Leo learned.

THIRTEEN

Writing – and the Shakespeare debate

There is a watershed in Tolstoy's life in a way: life before and after AK. Before AK, In War and Peace *and* Anna Karenina, *Tolstoy produced two great novels. After AK, he had written some good novellas and short stories, along with a vast amount of polemical and biographical writing. But the author of* War and Peace *and* Anna Karenina *has gone.*

In this second phase of life, Tolstoy has not sat happily with the genius of other writers, revealing himself as intensely competitive. He famously said this of Dostoyevsky: 'I read Dostoyevsky and was amazed by the sloppy, artificial, contrived writing.' He challenged Turgenev to a duel – after which they didn't speak for seventeen years, while the vitriol he pours on Shakespeare, calling him 'insignificant and immoral', has left Tolstoy diminished in many people's eyes.

Yet at the same time, he wishes to destroy the whole literary edifice, and deny it any importance. So on one occasion recently, he declared himself more famous than Pushkin, Gogol, Shakespeare, Molière and all other writers in the world. And then said: 'So what?'

He and Dostoyevsky never met, both jealous of each other. Dostoyevsky was an upholder of orthodox faith, but there were other differences. Count Leo Tolstoy was a man of health and physical vitality; and a man who wrote at leisure. One of the only Russians granted freedom of speech, he was shown amazing tolerance by the authorities. Dostoyevsky, on the other hand, was a frail epileptic, of poor background. He wrote under greater pressure than Tolstoy, and had little time to polish or hone his work. Dostoyevsky had no freedom to write, and was sent to Siberia for a minor offence against censorship laws. His experience of slum life, weakness and poverty was authentic; Tolstoy's was more out of curiosity, and because he thought it was right.

Tolstoy's relationship with Turgenev had been much closer. Turgenev was born into a wealthy family, and the two men had travelled Europe together. But Tolstoy could not cope with Turgenev's love of Western Europe; and the lack of moral spine he discerned in him. Yet it had been the rejected Turgenev, who, on his deathbed, pleaded with Tolstoy to get back to his former ways: 'My friend, return to literature!' he said.

Some people think Tolstoy is healthier and more liberated in his imagination than he is in his preaching. I am interested to ask about writing; and of course, the famous Shakespeare controversy.

SP: I wanted to ask you about your early writings; some would say your greatest writings – *War and Peace, Anna Karenina*.

LT: I have forgotten almost my whole past, all my writings, and everything that has led me to the level of consciousness by which I now live.

SP: So has literature lost its way? Or is it just you that's changed.

LT: It is thought that the more the desires – and the more refined these desires – the better; and nothing shows this more clearly than the descriptive poetry, and especially the novels, of the last two centuries.

SP: Is it a question of how the heroes and heroines – who represent the ideals of virtue – are portrayed?

LT: Indeed. In most cases the men who are meant to represent something noble and lofty – from Childe Harold down to the latest heroes of Feuillet, Trollope, or Maupassant – are simply depraved sluggards, consuming in luxury the labour of thousands, and themselves doing nothing useful for anybody. And then the heroines are the mistresses, who in one way or another, afford more or less delight to these men; and who prove quite as idle as they, and equally ready to consume the labour of others by their luxury.

SP: Is this so for all characters in literature?

LT: I do not refer to the representations of really abstemious and industrious people one occasionally meets with in literature. I am speaking of the usual type that serves as an ideal to the masses: of the character that the majority of men and women are trying to resemble. I remember the difficulty (inexplicable to me at the time) that I experienced when I wrote novels, a difficulty with which I contended and with which I know all novelists now contend who have even the dimmest conception of what constitutes real moral beauty.

SP: And what was the difficulty?

LT: The difficulty of portraying a type taken from the upper classes both as ideally good and kind, and yet also true to life! To be true to life, any description of a man or woman of the upper, educated classes must show them in their usual surroundings – that is, in luxury, physical idleness and demanding much. Now, from a moral point of view such a person is undoubtedly objectionable. But it is necessary to represent this person in such a way that he may at least appear attractive. And novelists try so to do this; and I also tried.

SP: But it was hard.

LT: The attempt to make an immoral fornicator and murderer – whether duellist or soldier; that is, someone utterly useless, idly drifting and a fashionable buffoon – the attempt to make them appear attractive, requires much art and effort. However, the readers of novels are, for the most part, exactly such men; and therefore readily believe that these Childe Harolds, Onegins, Monsieurs de Camors are very excellent people.

SP: How do you respond to criticism?

LT: Today I received two letters: one containing an article by Merezhovsky criticizing me; and the other from a foreigner, a German, also criticizing me.

SP: And your reaction?

LT: I felt bad. And I wondered why it is that people feel the need to vilify and criticize others for their higher aspirations.

SP: Such attitudes are not unknown in you.

LT: Then I realized that although one cannot condone criticism, it is unavoidable, necessary and beneficial. Without such criticism, a person would get carried away with himself and become vain. His need to please public opinion would gradually divert him from working on his soul.

SP: You talk about yourself now.

LT: Undeserved hatred and contempt liberates us from caring about public opinion, and puts our attention on the only steadfast foundation of life: following one's conscience, God's will.

SP: And so onto Shakespeare, sir, towards whom you seem to show a great deal of hatred and contempt, if I may say so. Everyone else loves him; but you beg to differ.

LT: My disagreement with the established opinion about

Shakespeare is not the result of an accidental frame of mind, nor of a light-minded attitude toward the matter. On the contrary, it is the outcome of many years' repeated and insistent endeavours to harmonize my own views of Shakespeare, with those established amongst all civilized men of the Christian world.

SP: But you haven't managed that?

LT: I remember the astonishment I felt when I first read Shakespeare. I expected to receive a powerful aesthetic pleasure, but having read, one after the other, works regarded as his best – *King Lear*, *Romeo and Juliet*, *Hamlet* and *Macbeth* – not only did I feel no delight, but I felt an irresistible repulsion and tedium! And I had to wonder: was I the one who was senseless in feeling works regarded as the summit of perfection by the whole of the civilized world, to be trivial and positively bad; or, was the significance which the civilized world attributes to the works of Shakespeare, itself senseless?

SP: You are not averse to disagreeing with the world.

LT: My consternation was increased by the fact that I have always felt keenly the beauties of poetry in every form. So why then should artistic works recognized by the whole world as those of a genius – the works of Shakespeare – not only fail to please me, but be disagreeable to me?

SP: Did you find the answer?

LT: For a long time, I could not believe in myself, and so during fifty years, in order to test myself, I several times recommenced reading Shakespeare in every possible form – in Russian, in English, in German and in Schlegel's translation, as I was advised. Several times I read the dramas and the comedies and historical plays, and I invariably underwent the same feelings: repulsion, weariness, and bewilderment. At the present time, being desirous once more to test myself, I have, as an old man again read the whole of Shakespeare, including the historical plays, the *Henrys*, *Troilus and Cressida*, the *Tempest*, *Cymbeline* – and do you know what?

SP: I think I can guess.

LT: I have felt, with even greater force, the same feelings! This time, however, feelings not of bewilderment, but a firm and indubitable conviction that the glory and genius attributed to Shakespeare unquestioningly – and which compels writers of our time to imitate him and readers and spectators to discover in him non-existent merits, thereby distorting their aesthetic and ethical understanding – is a great evil, as is every untruth.

Tolstoy then dismantles King Lear, *piece by piece. Being unacquainted with it myself, I do not pass comment. Like a dog putting down a gnawed bone, Tolstoy finally ceases talk of the play, having made the whole thing appear entirely absurd.*

LT: Such is this celebrated drama! However absurd it may appear in my rendering – which I have endeavoured to make as impartial as possible – I may confidently say that in the original, it is yet more absurd. For any man of our time – if he were not under the hypnotic suggestion that this drama is the height of perfection – it would be enough to read it to its end, if he had sufficient patience. He would then be convinced that far from being the height of perfection, it is a very bad, carelessly composed production, which – if it could have been of interest to a certain public at a certain time – can not now evoke among us anything but aversion and weariness. And what is more –

SP: Can there be more?

LT: Every reader of our time, who is free from the influence of suggestion, will also receive exactly the same impression from all the other extolled dramas of Shakespeare, not to mention the senseless, dramatized tales like *Pericles*, *Twelfth Night*, *The Tempest*, *Cymbeline*, and *Troilus and Cressida*. But sadly, such free-minded individuals, not inoculated with Shakespeare-worship, are no longer to be found in our Christian society. Every man of our society and time, from the first period of his conscious life, has been inoculated with the idea that Shakespeare is a genius, a poet and a dramatist, and that all his writings are the height of perfection.

SP: Doesn't he do character well?

LT: In reading Shakespeare's dramas, I was, from the very first, instantly convinced that he was lacking in the most important, if not the only, means of portraying characters which is individuality of language; the style of speech of every person being natural to his character. This is absent from Shakespeare.

SP: But Falstaff's good fun, isn't he?

LT: Falstaff is, indeed, quite a natural and typical character; but then it is perhaps the only natural and typical character depicted by Shakespeare. And this character is natural and typical because, of all Shakespeare's characters, it alone speaks a language proper to itself. And it speaks thus because it speaks in that same Shakespearian language, full of mirthless jokes and unamusing puns which, being unnatural to all Shakespeare's other characters, is quite in harmony with the boastful, distorted and depraved character of the drunken Falstaff. For this reason alone does this figure truly represent a definite character. Unfortunately, the artistic effect of this character is spoilt by the fact that it is so repulsive by its gluttony, drunkenness, debauchery, rascality, deceit and cowardice, that it is difficult to share the feeling of gay humour with which the author treats it. Thus it is with Falstaff.

SP: But I know many of our leading actors love to do his plays. Some say it is the height of their profession.

LT: Shakespeare, himself an actor, and an intelligent man, knew how to express by the means not only of speech, but of exclamation, gesture and the repetition of words, states of mind and developments; or changes of feeling taking place in the persons represented. This gives good actors the possibility of demonstrating their powers; which is often mistaken by critics for the expression of character. But however strongly the play of feeling may be expressed in one scene, a single scene can not give the character of a figure, when this figure – after a correct exclamation or gesture – begins in a language not its own, at the author's arbitrary will, to volubly utter words which are neither necessary nor in harmony with its character.

SP: But like many people, I own a book of Shakespeare's greatest lines and sayings. And they're wonderful!

LT: Thoughts and sayings may be appreciated in a prose work, or in an essay, or in a collection of aphorisms – but not in an artistic dramatic production, the object of which is to elicit sympathy with that which is represented. Therefore the monologues and sayings of Shakespeare, even did they contain very many deep and new thoughts, which they do not, do not constitute the merits of an artistic, poetic production. On the contrary, these speeches, expressed in unnatural conditions, can only spoil artistic works.

SP: So what is the first requirement of an artistic work?

LT: An artistic, poetic work – particularly a drama – must first of all excite in the reader or spectator the illusion that whatever the person represented is living through, or experiencing, is lived through or experienced by himself. Shakespeare is devoid of this feeling. His characters continually do and say what is not only unnatural to them, but utterly unnecessary.

SP: And unless I'm mistaken, it's not just literary style. Isn't it also that you find Shakespeare the man immoral?

LT: The subject of Shakespeare's pieces is the lowest, most vulgar view of life. It is a view which regards the external elevation of the lords of the world as a genuine distinction; and which despises the crowd – that is, the working classes. It repudiates not only all religious, but also all humanitarian, strivings directed to the betterment of the existing order. And the most important condition, sincerity, is completely absent in all Shakespeare's works. In all of them, one sees intentional artifice; one sees that he is not *in earnest*, but that he is merely playing with words. What then signifies the great fame these works have enjoyed for more than a hundred years?

SP: I appreciate your time on this subject. I know it is a discussion you have had many times before.

LT: Yes, many times during my life I have had occasion to argue about Shakespeare with his admirers; not only with people insensitive to poetry, but also with those who keenly felt poetic beauty, such as Turgenev, Fet and others. And every time, I encountered one and the same attitude toward my objection to the praises of Shakespeare. I was not refuted when I pointed out Shakespeare's defects; not at all! They said only that they were sorry at my lack of comprehension, and urged upon me the necessity of recognizing the extraordinary supernatural grandeur of Shakespeare. They did not explain to me in what the beauties of Shakespeare consisted; instead, they were just vaguely and exaggeratedly enraptured with the whole of Shakespeare, extolling some favourite passages:

the unbuttoning of Lear's button; Falstaff's lying – or Lady Macbeth's ineffaceable spots!

FOURTEEN
The end game

We sit in the garden. I am not sure how to begin this session. The air is warm, and a bee buzzes by. Tolstoy seems unusually content. I am to leave tomorrow morning, but wish to address the subject of death. Tolstoy is himself an old man; so how does he feel about the end game?

Not that death is new to him; far from it. His mother died when he was two; and try as he might, he could never get a mental picture of her. He saw little of his father, but recalls him with admiration and affection. He died in 1837, when Tolstoy was nine. Aunt Toinette was a mother substitute, but by the time we talk, his aunt is long gone, and he has lost his three brothers, Sergey, Dimitry and Nikolay. Six of his thirteen children are also dead. They say the death of their dear Vanya, aged seven, brought Tolstoy and Sofya together for a while.

Tolstoy moves gently on his rocking chair in the porch; a permitted luxury.

LT: I love it when you do not exult and rejoice alone in nature, but when around you, myriads of insects buzz and whirl, and beetles, clinging together, creep about – and all around you birds overflow with song!

SP: A picture of heaven, perhaps, and with your permission, I'd like to speak this afternoon about the afterlife.

LT: The afterlife? It is time to wake up, that is, to die. I already sometimes feel this awakening to another more real reality.

SP: I know that you see death as a time of transition. Is this so for everyone? You have lost children.

LT: People are born and live, in God's likeness; therefore they cannot exist without God nor can they be destroyed. They can be hidden from our eyes but not destroyed. Life is indestructible. It exists outside time and space; therefore, death can only change the form life takes in this world.

SP: Your daughter Masha died when she was 39, with pneumonia. Some say she was your favourite child; and perhaps the one most devoted to you. What was your experience at that time?

LT: It's strange but I didn't feel horror or fear; and nor did I feel that something unusual was taking place. I didn't even feel sorry or sad.

SP: That must have been strange?

LT: I seemed to think it necessary to evoke a feeling of sadness and I succeeded, but in the depths of my soul I was calmer than I would have been in the face of someone else's unkind or inconsiderate actions.

SP: Why do you think that was so? After all, this was the death of a child you loved.

LT: It was a physical phenomenon and therefore impersonal. I kept looking at her the whole time she was dying; it was amazingly peaceful. I thought of her as a being whose unfolding was occurring before my own. I closely watched her unfolding and felt happy. But the portion of her unfolding which was occurring in this world, stopped; in other words, I could no longer see the process; but that which unfolded, exists.

SP: Where?

LT: 'Where?' 'When?' These are questions which relate to the process of development here and cannot be used to refer to true, non spatial and non-temporal life.

SP: Your brother Sergei died of throat and tongue cancer. He was a resolute non-believer, but you were there at his death.

LT: Sergei died quietly without showing any sign – at least any obvious sign – that he was aware he was dying. It is a mystery, and whether it is good or bad I cannot say. He was incapable of active religious feeling – I might be wrong, but I don't think so. Nevertheless, he is all right. Something new and better has revealed itself as it has to me. A person's level of enlightenment is precious and important, but at what point it comes in the eternal cycle is unimportant. We often try to conceive our own deaths and our transition to the beyond, but it is impossible, just as it is impossible to fully comprehend God. The only thing we can trust is that death is good – as are all things that come from God.

SP: Eternity gives meaning to everything?

LT: If there is a God and future life, then such things as truth and goodness exist; and man's greatest happiness is in working to attain them. We have to live, to love and to believe that we do not live only in the moment on this little clump of earth, but that we lived and will live eternally in everything.

SP: And begin to understand our life as something greater than a brief wave in the ocean of time?

LT: People will know that they do not die, only when they understand that they were never born – but that they always existed and will exist. People will only believe in their immortality when they understand that their life is not a 'wave', but is eternal movement, which only appears as an individual wave in this life.

SP: But to go back a little, you had a great fear of death. What was the nature of that fear?

LT: The fear of death stems from a person mistakenly identifying his life with one limited part of it.

SP: But now death for you is merely the arrival of a new way of looking at the world?

LT: Death means the destruction of the physical organs I use to apprehend the world as it appears in this life. Death is the destruction of the glass through which I looked; and its replacement by another.

SP: There does seem to be something inside us suggesting immortality. I suppose the cynics will say it is the voice of delusion.

LT: The voice that tells us that we are immortal is the voice of God.

FIFTEEN

What then must we do?

What Then Must We Do? – *the title of one of Tolstoy's best polemical pieces – was for him, the only question worth asking. All other theological discussion was irrelevant, to which he was inclined to say: 'Well, so what?'*

There is nobility in this ideal. He wishes for everything to be practical; to result in better behaviour on earth. But like others before me, I have been surprised at the behaviour in the household. Someone said that the more Tolstoy tried to be like Jesus, the more unpleasant he became; that he may have been thinking holy thoughts, but behaved like 'a prosecutor and hang man', whether towards church leaders, government leaders, literary rivals – or his wife.

Perhaps the saint at home is his greatest challenge; and certainly Tolstoy has not tried to hide anything from me. Sofya is showing clearly signs of hysteria and paranoia; which are only made worse by her well-founded suspicions that Tolstoy and Chertkov are working on a secret new will, behind her back. Chertkov is clearly the apple of his eye, and Sofya the bane of his life, and they argue all the time.

LT: When an individual passes from one period of life to another, a time comes when he cannot go on in senseless activity and excitement as before. And in the same way, a similar time must come in the growth and development of humanity.

SP: And we have reached it now?

LT: I believe that such a time has now arrived, in that the

inherent contradiction of human life has now reached an extreme degree of tension. On the one side there is the consciousness of the beneficence of the law of love, and on the other, the existing order of life which has for centuries occasioned an empty, anxious, restless and troubled mode of life – conflicting as it does with the law of love and built on the use of violence. This contradiction must be faced, and the solution will clearly not be favourable to the outlived law of violence; but rather, to the truth which has dwelt in the hearts of men from remote antiquity: for the truth that the law of love is in accord with the nature of man.

SP: And the law of love asks that we free ourselves from both bad religion and bad science?

LT: If only people freed themselves from their beliefs in all kinds of Ormuzds and Brahmas, and their incarnation as Krishnas and Christs! Freed themselves from beliefs in heavens and hells, and in reincarnations and resurrections; from belief in the interference of the gods in the external affairs of the universe, and above all – if they freed themselves from belief in the infallibility of all the various Vedas, Bibles, Gospels, Korans and the like.

SP: That's a lot of religion to escape from.

LT: And let people free themselves also from blind belief in a variety of scientific teachings about infinitely small atoms and molecules; and in all the infinitely great and infinitely remote worlds, their movements and origin; as well as from faith in the infallibility of the scientific law to which humanity is at present subjected: the historic law, the economic laws, the law of struggle and survival, and so on – if people only freed themselves from this terrible accumulation of futile exercises of our lower capacities of mind and memory called the 'Sciences' – freed themselves from all this harmful, stupefying ballast

– the simple law of love, natural to man, accessible to all and solving all questions and perplexities, would of itself become clear and obligatory.

SP: So if we let go of false ways, the truth will come naturally to us?

LT: Indeed. Free your mind from those overgrown, mountainous imbecilities which hinder your recognition of it, and at once the truth will emerge from amid the pseudo-religious nonsense that has been smothering it: the indubitable, eternal truth inherent in man, which is one and the same in all the great religions of the world. It will in due time emerge and make its way to general recognition, and the nonsense that has obscured it will disappear of itself, and with it will go the evil from which humanity now suffers.

SP: That's a big call. What would be your first step?

LT: Try the experiment of ceasing to commit cruel, treacherous and base actions that you are constantly committing in order to maintain your position, and you will lose it at once. Try the simple experiment, as a government official, of giving up lying, and refusing to take part in executions and acts of violence; as a priest, of giving up deception; as a soldier, of giving up murder; as landowner or manufacturer, of giving up defending your property by fraud or force; and you will at once lose the position which you pretend is forced upon you, and which seems burdensome to you.

SP: We complain about our moral predicament but don't do anything to change it?

LT: A man cannot be placed against his will in a situation opposed to his conscience. If you find yourself in such a position it is not because it is necessary to anyone whatever; but simply because you wish it.

SP: So everyone should stop doing what they're doing. But wouldn't everything fall apart?

LT: I do not say if you are a landowner you are bound to give up your lands immediately to the poor; if a capitalist or manufacturer, your money to your work people; or if you are a tsar, minister, official, judge or general, you are bound to renounce immediately the advantages of your position; or if you are a soldier, on whom all the system of violence is based, to refuse immediately to obey in spite of all the dangers of insubordination. If you do so, you will be doing the best thing possible. But it may happen, and it is most likely, that you will not have the strength to do so. You have relations, a family, subordinates and superiors; you are under an influence so powerful you cannot shake it off. But you can always recognize the truth, and refuse to tell a lie about it.

SP: So even if I carry on doing wrong; I can at least avoid pretending that it's right?

LT: You can always avoid lying in this way to yourself and to others, and you ought to do so; because the one aim of your life ought to be to purify yourself from falsehood and to confess the truth. And you need only do that and your situation will change directly of itself. There is one thing, and only one thing, in which it is granted to you to be free in life, all else being beyond your power; that is to recognize and profess the truth.

SP: I just need to get up in the morning, and acknowledge what's true.

LT: The sole meaning of life is to serve humanity by

contributing to the establishment of the kingdom of God, which can only be done by the recognition and profession of the truth by every man.

SP: Some people say you advocate anarchy.

LT: I am not advocating anarchy.

SP: But you promote resistance to government.

LT: I live according to the teaching of the eternal law that does not permit aggression or participation in it. Does adherence to this law result either in anarchy or slavery under the yolk of, say, the Japanese or Germans? I do not know and I do not care to know.

SP: But do you seriously think non-resistance will change things? The world doesn't work like that.

LT: I have never expected that if we present the other cheek to a person who slaps us that this person will realize the error of his ways and stop hitting us; or understand the significance of our action. On the contrary, he will think and say: 'I did the right thing to hit him. The fact that he did not resist shows that he feels guilty and admits my superiority.' But even though I know this, I still think it is better for oneself and for everyone to turn the other cheek. This is the greatest joy. And then you will experience gratitude for an apparent misfortune.

SP: Self-induced misfortune? I don't see a queue forming.

LT: Only the conditions which we label misfortunes initiate the soul's struggle with the body and therefore, offer the real possibility of real life. Life itself, if we struggle consciously, is victorious; that is, the soul is victorious over the body.

SP: And your rational approach to life allows us a soul? That sounds surprisingly religious.

LT: We call 'soul' that which gives us life, and which we know within ourselves, in our limited and therefore imperfect bodies. We call 'God' that which is unbounded and therefore perfect. Life consists in striving for unification with that form from which we have been separated: unity with other souls and with God; with his perfection.

SP: And is the soul that which puts humans above other forms of life?

LT: While out walking, I clearly and sharply felt the inner life of cattle, sheep, moles, trees; each one somehow instinctively fulfilling its role, breeding in the summer pastures. The seed becomes the fir tree; the acorn becomes the oak tree, and they will grow and live centuries and produce new ones, as will the moles and sheep and people. And all this will occur into eternity and is happening in Africa, in India, in Australia and in every corner of the planet. And there are thousands and millions of such planets. When you clearly comprehend all this, talking about the grandeur of human affairs or even humans themselves is so much nonsense.

SP: Forgive me, but a turnip could not have written *War and Peace*.

LT: Yes, mankind is greater in comparison with the creatures we know, but just as there is an infinite number of beings lower than human beings, there must be an infinite number of higher beings who we do not know, because we cannot. Under such circumstances, for humans to speak about their greatness is laughable. The only thing one can ask of oneself, as a human being, is not to do stupid things. Yes, only that.

SP: What must we then do?

LT: Our job here is to regard ourselves as tools which the owner uses for a purpose we do not know. We must keep ourselves in fine form. So that if I am a plough, the metal should be sharp; if I am an oil lamp, I should keep burning. We are not told what is being accomplished in our lives; nor do we need to know.

SP: We trust.

LT: Take thought, and have faith in the gospel, in whose teaching is your happiness. If you do not take thought, you will perish just as the men perished, slain by Pilate, or crushed by the Tower of Siloam; as millions of men have perished, slayers and slain, executing and executed, torturers and tortured alike, and as the man foolishly perished, who filled his granaries full, and made ready for a long life, and died the very night that he planned to begin his life. Take thought and have faith in the Gospel, Christ said 1800 years ago; and he says it with even greater force now that the calamities foretold by him have come to pass, and the senselessness of our life has reached the furthest point of suffering and madness.

Suddenly Tolstoy looks tired; and the old man that he is. A chill night wind blows through the window. I shiver a little; perhaps summer is drawing to a close; and perhaps society as we know it also.

SP: Revolutionaries will inevitably take power in this country; it can't stagger on as it does now. Incidents of violence increase daily; what exists cannot hold.

LT: Yes, and when the revolutionaries take power, they will inevitably act the same way that those in power do now. In other words, they will use force, without which control over others cannot exist.

SP: And that doesn't concern you?

LT: I did what I could; let those who can, do better. It is very important to keep this in mind.

SP: Thank you, sir. And good night.

SIXTEEN
The following day…

My time is up, and I am leaving Yasnaya Polyana. Unfortunately, I leave Sofya and Leo in dispute. Once again, they are arguing over his literary estate, which she believes he is giving away to Chertkov.

'This proves there is a conspiracy against me!' she says.

'What do you mean, conspiracy?'

'Your diary has been given to Chertkov!'

'No, Sasha has it.'

I don't hear any more, but as my carriage lurches and rattles down the rutted drive way, I am put in mind of Tolstoy's novella, Father Sergius. *In this story, there proves to be a gaping chasm between the ideals of the priest and his actual behaviour: 'Our feet have reached holy places, but our hearts may not have done so,' says one character.*

As I journey home, I reflect on these words, thinking them a good epitaph for Leo Tolstoy. And as the man himself said, just because he walked the road like a drunk, didn't make it the wrong road.

SEVENTEEN
Afterword

Tolstoy died in Astopovo railway station, November 7th 1910. No one knows where he was bound. He had come from seeing his sister, Marya, in the convent at Shamardino. On his death, the church forbade her to pray for his soul, as he had died a heretic. But Marya continued to pray, saying: 'God grant that everyone may believe as strongly as he did.' The last two surviving children, Marya and Leo, had enjoyed a strong bond.

Tolstoy's death was a global event. There were student demonstrations in university towns across the British Empire, and rallies against the death penalty. There were 4000 mourners at Yasnaya Polyana, when his coffin returned there.

He was buried on November 9th; on the edge of the ravine in Zakaz Wood. It was here, all those years before, that his eldest brother Nikolay had buried the green stick, on which was written the secret of world harmony; a secret and a search that was to dominate Tolstoy's life.

It was the first public funeral since the conversion of Russia by St. Vladimir not to include religious rites; the church refused to allow them. The crowd sang old Russian hymns nonetheless, in a public outpouring of grief, never previously seen for a novelist. But then of course, he wasn't being honoured as a novelist. He was being honoured for something else.

It was said that most of the mourners had never heard of *War and Peace*. But they had read the writings of a prophet. In this same year, Rasputin urged the Empress to dissolve the Duma, the Russian parliament. The end of the old order was well underway.

Simon Parke

Simon Parke was a priest in the Church of England for twenty years, before leaving for fresh adventures. He worked for three years in a supermarket, stacking shelves and working on the till. He was also chair of the shop union. He has since left to go free lance, and now writes, leads retreats and offers consultancy.

He has written for *The Independent* and *The Evening Standard*, and is currently columnist with the *Daily Mail*. His weekly supermarket diary, 'Shelf Life', ran for 15 months in the *Mail on Saturday*, and he now contributes another weekly column called 'One-Minute Mystic.' The book version of *Shelf Life* has recently been published by Rider. The book version of *One-Minute Mystic* is published by Hay House in January 2010.

Other books by Simon include *Forsaking the Family* – a refreshingly real look at family life. Our families made us; yet we understand very little of how our experiences as children still affects us. The book starts by contemplating Jesus' ambivalence towards his own family, particularly his parents; reflects on how our family settings can both help and harm us; and suggests paths for freedom and authenticity.

The Beautiful Life – ten new commandments because life could be better was published by Bloomsbury, and describes ten skilful attitudes for life. Simon leads retreats around this book, and talks about it on this site. It is now also available in audio form with White Crow books.

Simon has been a teacher of the Enneagram for twenty years. The enneagram is an ancient and remarkable path of self-understanding, and Simon's book on the subject, published by Lion, is called *Enneagram – a private session with the world's greatest psychologist*.

Another bloody retreat is Simon's desert novel, describing events at the monastery of St James-the-Less set in the sands of Middle Egypt. It follows the fortunes of Abbot Peter and the rest of the community, when the stillness of their sacred setting is rudely and irrevocably shattered.

Simon was born in Sussex, but has lived and worked in London for twenty-five years. He has written comedy and satire for TV and radio, picking up a Sony radio award. He has two grown-up children and his hobbies include football, history and running. For more information, visit his website www.simonparke.com

Also available from White Crow Books

Marcus Aurelius—*The Meditations*
ISBN 978-1-907355-20-2

Elsa Barker—*Letters from a Living Dead Man*
ISBN 978-1-907355-83-7

Elsa Barker—*War Letters from the Living Dead Man*
ISBN 978-1-907355-85-1

Elsa Barker—*Last Letters from the Living Dead Man*
ISBN 978-1-907355-87-5

Richard Maurice Bucke—*Cosmic Consciousness*
ISBN 978-1-907355-10-3

G. K. Chesterton—*The Everlasting Man*
ISBN 978-1-907355-03-5

G. K. Chesterton—*Heretics*
ISBN 978-1-907355-02-8

G. K. Chesterton—*Orthodoxy*
ISBN 978-1-907355-01-1

Arthur Conan Doyle—*The Edge of the Unknown*
ISBN 978-1-907355-14-1

Arthur Conan Doyle—*The New Revelation*
ISBN 978-1-907355-12-7

Arthur Conan Doyle—*The Vital Message*
ISBN 978-1-907355-13-4

Arthur Conan Doyle with Simon Parke—*Conversations with Arthur Conan Doyle*
ISBN 978-1-907355-80-6

Leon Denis with Arthur Conan Doyle—*The Mystery of Joan of Arc*
ISBN 978-1-907355-17-2

The Earl of Dunraven—*Experiences in Spiritualism with D. D. Home*
ISBN 978-1-907355-93-6

Meister Eckhart with Simon Parke—*Conversations with Meister Eckhart*
ISBN 978-1-907355-18-9

Kahlil Gibran—*The Forerunner*
ISBN 978-1-907355-06-6

Kahlil Gibran—*The Madman*
ISBN 978-1-907355-05-9

Kahlil Gibran—*The Prophet*
ISBN 978-1-907355-04-2

Kahlil Gibran—*Sand and Foam*
ISBN 978-1-907355-07-3

Kahlil Gibran—*Jesus the Son of Man*
ISBN 978-1-907355-08-0

Kahlil Gibran—*Spiritual World*
ISBN 978-1-907355-09-7

Hermann Hesse—*Siddhartha*
ISBN 978-1-907355-31-8

D. D. Home—*Incidents in my Life Part 1*
ISBN 978-1-907355-15-8

Mme. Dunglas Home; edited, with an Introduction, by Sir Arthur Conan Doyle—*D. D. Home: His Life and Mission*
ISBN 978-1-907355-16-5

Andrew Lang—*The Book of Dreams and Ghosts*
ISBN 978-1-907355-97-4

Edward C. Randall—*Frontiers of the Afterlife*
ISBN 978-1-907355-30-1

Lucius Annaeus Seneca—*On Benefits*
ISBN 978-1-907355-19-6

Rebecca Ruter Springer—*Intra Muros—My Dream of Heaven*
ISBN 978-1-907355-11-0

W. T. Stead—*After Death* or *Letters from Julia: A Personal Narrative*
ISBN 978-1-907355-89-9

Leo Tolstoy, edited by Simon Parke—*Tolstoy's Forbidden Words*
ISBN 978-1-907355-00-4

Leo Tolstoy—*A Confession*
ISBN 978-1-907355-24-0

Leo Tolstoy—*The Gospel in Brief*
ISBN 978-1-907355-22-6

Leo Tolstoy—*The Kingdom of God is Within You*
ISBN 978-1-907355-27-1

Leo Tolstoy—*My Religion: What I Believe*
ISBN 978-1-907355-23-3

Leo Tolstoy—*On Life*
ISBN 978-1-907355-91-2

Leo Tolstoy—*Twenty-three Tales*
ISBN 978-1-907355-29-5

Leo Tolstoy—*What is Religion and other writings*
ISBN 978-1-907355-28-8

Leo Tolstoy—*Work While Ye Have the Light*
ISBN 978-1-907355-26-4

Leo Tolstoy with Simon Parke—*Conversations with Tolstoy*
ISBN 978-1-907355-25-7

Howard Williams with an Introduction by Leo Tolstoy—*The Ethics of Diet: An Anthology of Vegetarian Thought*
ISBN 978-1-907355-21-9

All titles available as eBooks, and select titles available in Audiobook format from www.whitecrowbooks.com

www.ingramcontent.com/pod-product-compliance
Lightning Source LLC
LaVergne TN
LVHW011205080426
835508LV00007B/608